WITHDRAWN
HARVARD LIBRARY
WITHDRAWN

Reaching and Teaching Children Who are Victims of Poverty

Reaching and Teaching Children Who are Victims of Poverty

Edited by
Alice Duhon-Ross

Symposium Series
Volume 55

The Edwin Mellen Press
Lewiston•Queenston•Lampeter

Library of Congress Cataloging-in-Publication Data

Reaching and teaching children who are victims of poverty / edited by Alice Duhon-Ross.
    p.   cm. -- (Symposium series ; v. 55)
    Includes bibliographical references.
    ISBN 0-7734-7964-3
    1. Poor children--Education--United States. 2. Educational equalization--United States. I. Duhon-Ross, Alice. II. Series: Symposium series (Edwin Mellen Press) ; v. 55.
LC4091.R38   1999
371.826' 942--dc21   99-26084
                                                                                CIP

This is volume 55 in the continuing series
Symposium Series
Volume 55 ISBN 0-7734-7964-3
SS Series ISBN 0-7734-989-X

A CIP catalog record for this book is available from the British Library.

Copyright © 1999   The Edwin Mellen Press

All rights reserved. For information contact

        The Edwin Mellen Press   The Edwin Mellen Press
               Box 450   Box 67
            Lewiston, New York   Queenston, Ontario
          USA 14092-0450   CANADA L0S 1L0

                      The Edwin Mellen Press, Ltd.
                      Lampeter, Ceredigion, Wales
                   UNITED KINGDOM SA48 8LT

                 Printed in the United States of America

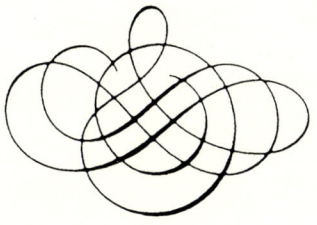

Reaching and Teaching Children Who Are Victims of Poverty

Table of Contents

Preface		V
Acknowledgements		VII
Introduction		IX
Chapter 1:	Reaching and Teaching Children Who are Victims of Poverty *Rose M. Duhon-Sells, Ph.D, The Union Institute, Cincinnati, Ohio, McNeese State University, Lake Charles Louisiana; Halloway C. Sells, Ph.D., The Union Institute, Cincinnati, Ohio & Glendolyn Jean Louis, Fonville Middle School, Houston, TX*	1
Chapter 2:	Teachers As Providers of Social Support to Help Prevent Child Abuse and Neglect: An Important Message for Educators to Convey *Brenda Burrell, University of New Orleans*	11
Chapter 3:	Making Connections in Science and Mathematics a Means To Motivate Minority Student *Shelbie M. Anderson Ph.D., University of Arkansas at Pine Bluff*	31
Chapter 4:	The Implications of Utilizing Eurocentric Constructs in the Education of Poor African American School Children *Michael E. Orok, Ph.D., Albany State University & Teresa Merriweather-Orok, Ph.D., Albany State University.*	49
Chapter 5:	Respectful Education for All Children *Barbara Trzcinske, Livonia, MI*	65
Chapter 6:	Assisting Poverty Stricken Students Through Early Identification, Sound Instructional Practices, and Modified Content Area Reading Strategies *Glynn Travis King Ph.D., Albany State University*	71

Chapter 7:	Attitudes and Experiences of College Students On Domestic Violence Renee Wallace, Ph.D., Albany State University	85
Chapter 8:	**Discovering the Potential of the "Whole Child"** Audrey W. Beard, Ed.D., Albany State University Melvin A. Shelton M.Ed., Albany State University	93
Chapter 9:	Providing Support For At-Risk Students In Higher Education Deborah E. Bembry, Ph.D. Albany State University Sylvia A. Bembry, Ph.D. Winston-Salem State University	103
Chapter 10:	Configuring Curriculum in low Socioeconomic Schools for Increasing Students Achievement Burrel Block, Ph.D., Albany State University	111
Chapter 11:	Instructional Strategies for Teachers Who Teach Students Who are Victims of Poverty Claude Perkins, Ph.D., Dean College of Education, Albany State University & Alice Duhon-Ross, Ph.D., Albany State University **Roslin Growe, Ph.D., University of Southwestern Louisiana**	129
Chapter 12:	Using the Whole–Language Approach with Minority Students Gwendolyn Duhon-Bordeaux, Ph.D., McNeese State University Katrina Boden-Webb, M.Ed., Grambling State University Jimmy McJamerson M.A. + 68	139
Chapter 13:	Literacy In The Early Years Phyllis C. Cuevas Ph.D., McNeese State University	147
Chapter 14:	At Risk Students, Who are They? Tony Manson, Ph.D., Pevy State University	153
Chapter 15:	From Under-Prepared To Academic Success; A Case Study For Student Athlete Support Programs Craig Curry M.Ed., Albany State University	159
Chapter 16:	Educational Programs Turning Victims Into Survivors Jerry Hardee, Ph.D., Vice President of Academic Affairs Albany State University, Alice Duhon-Ross Ph.D, & Ethelyn Lumpkin, Graduate Student, Albany State University	167

Chapter 17: The Full Service School: A Holistic Approach to   175
Effectively ServeChildren in Poverty
Beverly Watnick Ph. D., Miami-Dade County Public Schools
Arlene Sacks Ph.D., Union Institute

Chapter 18: Fate of the World's Children: A Global Challenge   193
Estela C. Matriano, Ed.D., Cincinnati, Ohio

Preface

America is viewed globally as one the richest most prosperous countries on this planet. Yet, according to the U.S. census bureaus, in 1992 over 42% of the school age children are victims of poverty. The victimization of these is enormous, including physical abuse, neglect and the pains of poverty. This book contains chapters focused on strategies and techniques for Educators to reach and teach these students victimized by poverty. The impoverish conditions of children in our schools negatively impact their total developmental process. It is difficult at best for children to grow to their fullest physical potential when they do not have adequate food and nutrition to supplement their growth. It is an awesome task for children in poverty to develop intellectually without early exposure to books, intellectual documentaries and opportunities to communicate with intelligent and educated adults. Children of this population suffer tremendously in the development of their socialization skills. Many have had limited basic experiences of celebrating birthdays, traveling across the state line, participating in extracurricular activities, such as dance classes, music classes or community sports.

Consequently classroom teachers have an awesome tasks of identifying these students' strengths and using those to strengthen their weaknesses. Fortunately, young children are resilient and are miraculously capable of blossoming to their fullest potential in spite of their impoverish circumstances. Schools can provide loving, caring, compassionate and affective teachers to help them to conceptualize life's possibilities. The classroom teachers for this population of students are often their only source of hope to rise above their impoverish conditions.

This task takes the entire school personnel including administrators, teachers, staff, custodians and lunchroom workers. For if all adults in the school environment are not in one accord and committed to appropriately meeting the academic needs, as well as provide for these children's emotional stability, the best efforts will not help the children to achieve academic success.

The following are suggestions educators may use to effectively meet the academic needs of impoverish children, such as;

1. Except children as they are and expect them to learn in spite of their impoverish circumstances.
2. Be careful not to blame the victim, children do not have the luxury of selecting the family in which they are born.
3. Celebrate the diversity that exist among children including; socioeconomic status, race, gender and cognitive styles.
4. Use positive discipline techniques to avoid attacking the student's sprit in a way that will cause them to academically shut down.
5. Educators need to communicate on a personal informal level daily with each child allowing them to experience a sense of belonging and to know that someone cares.

Thus, the content of this book Reaching and Teaching who Are Victims of Poverty will provide a body of knowledge for parents, teachers, administrators and individuals who are concerned about the appropriate academic development of all children.

Dr. Portia Holmes Shields
President, Albany State University
Albany, Georgia

Acknowledgements

My great appreciation goes to all the contributors of this book. A special thanks goes to the reviewers of the text, Onetta Williams, Ph.D. and James Paschall, Ph.D. whose contributions have been helpful, timely and professional.

A final and most heartfelt note of appreciation goes to my daughter Allison Rose and family. They have been very patient and loving during this process.

Introduction

The poverty rate for children in the United States exceeds that of all other Western, industrialized nations except Australia. Moreover, poverty among children has increased substantially since 1970, affecting more that one-fifth of all U.S. children. These persistent high rates require new ideas for both research and public policy. It's not secret that a glaring disparity exists in American education. Class and race play an enormous role in determining the quality of educational opportunities available to a child. There were twenty four authors and co-authors chosen to submit chapters for the text. The authors selected are among those who reflect the views that the poor themselves are not to blame for their poverty, and who challenge the position that the poor can achieve economic security by simply changing their values, behavior, or work ethic. The titles listed in this book take a critical look at the educational system serving the poor, and teaching methods that can be adopted by educators committed to improving the lives of the poor.

This text is designed to address a major problem that exist in the educational system nationally. There is a gap between the academic preparation of school personnel, administrators, counselors and classroom teachers, and that of the academic need of students who are victimized by poverty. Traditionally, the curriculum in teacher education programs focused on providing a body of knowledge appropriate to enable students to participate in an environment that utilizes the life experience skills developed within the boundaries of the middle class financial status. The educational system has many teachers who are ill-prepared to serve as facilitators or providers of guidance in helping these students structure the information they are exposed to daily in their impoverishment environment. They need help to process that into meaningful knowledge that they may use as tools to help them benefit from the academic information provided in the school setting.

The authors of this book are committed to providing information that will stimulate the thinking and create a desire which will motivate all constituencies in the educational arena to change the course of the educational infrastructure in an effort to save students who may be lost due to their life circumstance. A brief outline of those chapters are as follows:

Chapter 1 will focus on strategies and techniques such as learning to understand how to manage and utilize their feelings to enhance their economic progress. Children who are victimized by poverty often have a difficult time making the transition from home culture to school culture because of the impact of their life experiences.

Chapter 2 is written for teacher educators and provides information about the relationships between (a) child abuse/neglect and poverty and (b) child abuse/neglect and education.

Chapter 3 focuses on helping teachers to make the connections in science and mathematics as a means to motivate minority students.

Chapter 4 will focus on the nature of education available to minority children in the United States.

Chapter 5 discusses the importance of honoring, motivating and respecting children and families equally by adequately meeting their individual needs. Suggestions are provided for creating positive school and classroom environments to assist children of poverty in their learning.

Chapter 6 provides classroom teachers with practical advice and usable techniques to aid in connecting with and providing success for low-income students.

Chapter 7 examines attitudes and experiences of college students on domestic violence.

Chapter 8 will demonstrate how teachers can incorporate children's learning styles and multiple intelligence's as the cornerstone of their instruction.

Chapter 9 demonstrates how using large classroom instruction to teach is efficient but not effective for most students. Issues are addressed such as paring at-risk students with peer mentors can go a long way in improving not only academic but social and emotional development.

Chapter 10 will provide in detail the various configurations of low socioeconomic schools that have been successful in helping students achieve at higher levels. The impact of small pupil/teacher ratios on learning, the impact of well-trained teachers, and the impact of several programs will be considered. The author will explore ways that learning need not be a function of wealth.

Chapter 11 will focus on classroom management approaches and instructional strategies viewed effective for working with children who are victims of poverty.

Chapter 12 discusses the whole-language approach to teaching reading and provide documentation as to how students are positively impacted when reading stories about people from the similar ethnic backgrounds as they are.

Chapter 13 addresses how educators can teach literacy skills to children in the early years and the impact parents have on children's attitudes about reading.

Chapter 14 examines a history of the treatment and consideration given in American education to students who are now classified as at-risk.

Chapter 15 examines how athletes support programs provides directions for student athletics.

Chapter 16 provides descriptions of successful academic educational programs that changed the life course of many students who are victimized by impoverishment circumstances.

Chapter 17 examines issues impacting children in poverty and their chances for success in life, and how one can lead to the conclusion that there is a critical need for a central point where active collaboration between schools, families and communities can take place.

Chapter 18 examines the state of the world's children, which has determined their fate in the global village.

This text will be invaluable to students, teachers, administrators, teacher educators, and community members who are interested in providing quality education for all children, especially those children who are victimized by poverty

Alice Duhon-Ross

Editor

Chapter One

**REACHING AND TEACHING CHILDREN
WHO ARE VICTIMS
OF POVERTY**

Rose M. Duhon-Sells, Ph.D.
The Union Institute
Cincinnati, Ohio
McNese State University
Lake Charles, Louisiana

Halloway C. Sells, Ph.D.
The Union Institute
Cincinnati, Ohio

Glendolyn Jean Louis
Fonville Middle School
Houston, Texas

America has over forty percent 40% of her school age children who are victimized by poverty. This is a condition for which children have no control and the condition controls every aspect of their lives. Unfortunately, children were not given a choice, even though, they are often blamed for their victimization.

The sad dilemma is that these children do not have access to the quality of education necessary to develop the essential skill for them to experience academic success. The ironic part of this situation is that the rationale for this type thinking is that the individuals are in denial because the truth would cause a very high level of guilt feelings.

In the Fall of 1997, I had the opportunity of working with a group of ninth graders at a local high school. I met with this group of students Tuesday afternoon from 1:00 to 02:30 p.m. We worked on self-science skills such as, self-awareness, self-concept, strategies and techniques to resolve conflict, tips on how to manage their anger, and appropriate behavior for various social settings.

There were days that we worked the whole period that I was there and other days we just talked about life issues. One of the most exciting topics we discussed was college life. Also, they lit up when we talked about male/female relationships which created a perfect opportunity for me to share with them the importance of the responsibility that accompanies intimate relationships. There were other days when they arrived at the session very frustrated because of some incident where the teacher disrespected them or discriminated against them by treating them like they were totally insignificant.

Consequently, the second week of the project the group was very playful and I was getting stressed out, beginning to think that my work was in vain. Then, one student made a comment that totally changed my thinking. She said to the group, " listen guys, if we don't start listening Dr. Sells will quit coming to meet with us and I enjoy meeting with her, so you better stop ". That comment helped me to realize that those students really needed someone to care about them and their future and they enjoyed having someone they viewed as a professional to listen and interact with them on a weekly basis. Immediately, I realized that often students in the inner city are forced to project an attitude of not caring, this serves as a defense mechanism and a survival tool to function effectively in spite of the victimization of poverty they are confronted with on a daily basis. The pressure this group of students had to deal with in school, at home, and in the community would kill the spirit of the average human being at a paralyzing level.

It is crucial that classroom teachers be prepared academically to provide appropriate instructional strategies to reach and teach this growing population of students who are victimized by poverty. The new paradigm that is essential must include learning activities that integrate technology, the human spirit, and cognitive development. In order to ensure that the educational system is providing an equal opportunity for this group of students to earn an excellent educational experience is a major challenge for policy makers, school administrators, and educators. Unfortunately, this isn't a major issue on the discussion table for most school boards in America.

Politics, greed, and racism are major obstacles in the educational arena for children who are victims of poverty. Therefore, the curriculum offerings are often irrelevant to the impoverishment student because their life experiences are not addressed in the average curriculum. Research has shown that learning occurs through association. Piaget states is his research that learning occurs through association and accommodation and students draw from the knowledge acquired from the home environment to experience success in the school environment. Unfortunately, for poor children the home environment and the school environment are totally different and one is deliberately isolated from the other pretending that all children are coming from average income families.

There must be continuity between home and school life even though the home conditions for children who are victims of poverty have limited resources professional educators must take the first step to make the connection through a relevant curriculum. Carl Grant, (1994) states that student's academic success often becomes a deciding factor in their life accomplishments, societal contributions, and healthy fully functioning adults.

Many successful citizens have come from impoverished circumstances as children but someone helped them to realize their work. Educators must strive and constantly assess their biases and prejudices in order to move beyond looking at students through the eyes of the myth that says poor children are responsible for their poverty.

Teacher expectation is a key element in helping impoverished students to develop thinking about themselves that is greater than their present circumstances. Educators need to help these students to develop a vision whereby they can see themselves rising above their present circumstances and becoming successful, contributing citizens of these United States.

The designer of the school curriculum must be cognizant of the various societal factors that are currently impacting the lives of students who are victims of poverty, such as, family violence, drug and alcohol abuse, and often adult depression. There is a world prime for a new paradigm in the teaching and learning process that will address the unique problems of children who are victimized by poverty. This curriculum must include instructional strategies that will consider the mind sets, body of knowledge these children acquire within the neighborhood in the community and from the negativism in the media about poverty stricken people.

The curriculum must reflect the elements in the students lives that are important to them. They must be accepted, appreciated, and acknowledged as meaningful learners with unique qualities.

The educators must assume the awesome responsibilities to become educators committed to providing learning experiences for students that will meet them where are intellectually and help them to grow to their fullest potential. They must be willing to spend time on task and learn about these student's personal lives, background experiences, life structure and culture. Those are essential skills prior to making decisions about what, how, and why the content of the school curriculum should be.

Currently, research shows that the educational system in this country has failed in their effort to provide access to excellence in education for the masses. A large number of impoverished students who have gone through the motion of twelve (12) years of school can neither read nor write at a level of literacy. This is a concern for all human beings on the face of the earth because we are very interdependent on each other. The knowledge, life skills, and expertise of one person may become the saving grace of us all.

The major thrust of a curriculum designed to meet the unique needs of impoverished students are as follows:

1) knowledge of the life experiences of this student population;
2) knowledge of current research as to how to best use technology to improve the teaching and learning process by utilizing the current knowledge of impoverished children;
3) knowledge of this population of students interests, desires, learning styles, and

academic strengths;

4) knowledge of the academic preparation, multi cultural experiences and commitment of the teachers responsible for providing a valid teaching and learning process that will reach and teach all students specifically students who are victims of poverty;

5) knowledge of local resources available for these students and their families as a tool to help students to learn the quality of their worth.

The most important element of the curriculum is the implementation of the Peace Education Thrust helping students to know that poverty wasn't designed as their life's destiny. The level of violence and conflict in poor neighborhoods will only grow without the implementation of a Peace Education Program at all educational levels to encourage all students to strive to recapture school safety and to discourage youth violence and hate crimes.

The technological nature of this era has created a infrastructure that demands national communication and collaboration. The designing of curriculum and instructional strategies must focus on using technology to reach students who are victims of poverty by integrating their life experience into the new paradigm for effective educational programs to meet the unique needs of students who are living in neighborhoods that cause them to feel hopeless and helpless about their futures.

The key in the equation is the knowledge as to how to best utilize and strengthen the human spirit, which is the glue that holds together the total curriculum and is often the determining factor of a child's academic success.

The technologically demonstrated school system is widening the gap between the haves and the haves not. Many impoverished children do not have access to the current technologically equipment that is available in the schools and in the homes of their classrooms. Unfortunately, their parents are totally illiterate about computers and are often intimidated by any form of technology. Consequently, these students will be expected to compete in classes with students who have computers in their homes and where technology is a part of their daily lives.

The educators who are committed, dedicated, and determined to ensure impoverished students access to educational excellence will create evening computer classes for students and their parents and they will make home visits with lap-top computers to help parents confront their fears of computers and develop the basic skills to be able to communicate with their children the importance and pleasure of working with technology. This educator will also work with community leaders to provide computers in local community centers.

The technological knowledge of this group of students may be the determining factors as to whether they grow up to be an asset or a deficits to society.

The impoverished conditions of students often attack the status of the human spirit. They are living in a society of plenty; the daily media shows people who are enjoying great luxuries. The illusion is that these people have everything they want just for the asking.

Little attention is focused on hard work; therefore, the thinking of some students is, "shall I accept the humiliation of attending school without the fashionable clothes or allow myself to invite my friends over to my home to be embarrassed by the condition of my home life". Unfortunately, they often seek external means, out of the school setting, to lift their spirits in order to emotionally feel better and they often end up in trouble with the authorities.

The academic curriculum must include opportunities for impoverished students to develop a strong positive sense of self-worth and use effective critical thinking skills. This will help them to have a vision of themselves one functioning day in the mainstream.

In 1979, Boyer defined the economically poor, disadvantaged learners and those who came from the following home conditions:

- Low-income families with a non-producing or marginally, producing bread winner;

- Low-income families who frequently reside in neighborhoods where dwellings are limited on lacking in structure (material from which they are made), in architecture and in maintenance;
- Low-income families who live in housing developments especially, constructed for low-income families;
- Low-income families who are often recipients of public financial assistance through social welfare agencies.

Boyer concluded that these students were victims of social alienation caused by racial, ethnic, or class discrimination with all of its accompanying aspirations in housing, employment, and education. Unfortunately, the impoverishment of that population of students has become processively worst within the past eighteen (18) years since the publication of Boyer's book entitled, Teaching the Economically Poor.

The curricula and instructional strategies have not changed at the university level where pre-service teachers are prepared nor in the K-12 school system where teachers are responsible for providing an educational experience for impoverished students.

The education curriculum today (1998) still offers instruction as though all the students were living in families that are financially stable. The present educational model was designed in the eighteenth (18th) century to educate white, middle class boys how to lead a segregated country. The results are clear...the failure of educating children who are victims of poverty.

In 1988, Kozol describes a different impoverished student population in his book, Rachel's and Her Children, Homeless Families in America. He refers to them as ordinary people, who have experienced hardships which resulted in homelessness. This book contains a series of stories of how society has failed many families with children. Consequently, the educational systems often appear to be in a state of denial by not adapting the teaching/learning process to the unique needs of improved learners.

There are over five hundred thousand (500,000) homeless people in America. Homeless people are poor people and their impoverished condition was not their choice. There are many critics who blame poor people for their circumstances and make stupid comments such as, "my grandparents were poor and they worked hard to overcome their poor conditions". When educators make those comments, it is a reflection of a lack of knowledge of current conditions of poverty in this country.

The poverty and homeless condition in America is predicted to expand to nineteen million by the Year 2003, according to a study funded by the Congress and carried out by M.I.T. Professor Phillip Clay.

Thus, this chapter is a world cry to national/state policy makers, educational leaders/administrators, and educators at all levels for a change in the teaching and learning process to include the experiences, hopes, and dreams of students who are victims of poverty.

Brazelton has identified seven key elements describing children's capacity to learn:

- Confidence. A sense of control and mastery of one's body, behavior, and world; The children's sense that he is more likely than not to succeed at what he undertakes, and that adults will be helpful.
- Curiosity. The sense that finding out about things is positive and leads to pleasure.
- Intentionality. The wish and capacity to have an impact and to act upon that with persistence. This is related to a sense of competence, of being effective.
- Self-Control. The ability to modulate and control one's own actions in age appropriate ways a sense of inner control.
- Relatedness. The ability to engage with others based on the sense of being understood by and understanding others.
- Capacity to Communicate. The wish and ability to verbally exchange ideas, feelings, and concepts with others. This related to a sense of trust in others

and of pleasure in engaging with others, including adults.
- Cooperativeness. The ability to balance one own needs with others in group activity. (Goleman, 1995)

The above essential characteristics for children to learn and grow are often not available in the environments of poverty stricken children. They are often growing in communities that stifle the developmental process of these children in every area. Unfortunately, parents of these children are experiencing pressure to survive and are often not mentally and emotionally strong enough to be aware of the impact of their family circumstances of the developmental process of their children. Many of them must work up to three (3) jobs paying minimum wages in order to provide food and shelter for their families.

The curriculum designers must be cognizant of the family situations of these students in order to provide instructional strategies, that ensures specific learning activities are focused on this population. In order for children to realize that their academic experience is capable of serving as a tool that builds the bridge to a better life.

References

Goleman, D. (1995), Emotional Intelligence, New York: Bantam Books.

Grant, Carl (1995) The National Association for Multicultural Education Conference Proceedings

Boyer, James (1982) Teaching the Economically Poor

Kozol, Janathan (1988) Rachel and Her Children Homeless Families in America

Chapter 2

Teachers As Providers of Social Support to Help
Prevent Child Abuse and Neglect: An Important Message for
Teacher Educators to Convey

Brenda Burrell
University of New Orleans
New Orleans, Louisiana

Many teachers who work in schools that are part of communities with low income not only witness consequences of poverty, but also see evidence of the devastation of abuse and neglect. The most powerful impact anyone can have on abuse and neglect is through prevention. No one can unkill a child or completely erase the profound and complex effects of abuse or neglect that does not result in death. Devastation begets devastation and the consequences of abuse and neglect intensifies, worsens, and spreads. Effective efforts to reach and teach students who are victims of poverty in ways that help them to emerge as survivors must include ways that address child abuse and neglect and must involve efforts to reach and teach their parents, families, and significant others.

Teacher educators are urged to incorporate information and discussions about child abuse and neglect into teacher preparation curricula, with at least three objectives in mind: (a) to increase teachers' knowledge and understanding about child abuse and neglect, including its relationship with poverty; (b) to acquaint teachers with their roles as mandated reporters of suspicions of child abuse and neglect; and (c) to help teachers develop awareness and skills related to ways they can help prevent child abuse and neglect. One way teachers can be proactive in helping to prevent child abuse and neglect is by being a social support for parents and other family members. As part of a pedagogical curriculum, teacher educators can direct their students to design and execute individualized professional development plans that specifically focus on enhancing competencies related to proactive intervention, like the prevention of child abuse and neglect.

Poverty and Child Abuse and Neglect

The epidemic status and devastating consequences of child abuse are long-standing, and; as many theorists suggests, generally attributable to a variety of complex and interrelated individual, family, social, and cultural factors. One of those factors that have been repeatedly associated with child abuse and neglect is poverty; and, both poverty levels and levels of child abuse and neglect are continuously escalating (Children's Defense Fund, 1997; Drake & Pandey, 199 6; McCurdy & Daro, 1994).

Child abuse and neglect is prevalent across all human boundaries. Victims and perpetrators of all types of abuse and neglect are found among people of all categories of any descriptor possible, including socioeconomic status. However, while all socioeconomic levels are represented among abusive and neglectful parents, the highest concentration of reports of abuse and neglect occur among the poor and among the poorest of the poor (Drake & Pandey, 1996; Garbarino & Sherman, 1980; Gil, 1969; Letourneau, 1981; Magnuson, 1983; United States Department of Health, Education, & Welfare, 1977; Wright, 1976). Webster-Stratton (1985) has found low family income to be one of the most significant variables discriminating between abusive and non abusive families.

In a study in which all of the participants were identified as being poor (living in a government-funded housing development and receiving government financial assistance), those who abused their children were the poorest of the poor (United States Department of Health, Education, & Welfare, 1977). In their study of community characteristics as predictors of abuse and neglect rates, Spearly and Lauderdale (1983) found that the higher the proportion of families with annual incomes over $15,000 in a certain county, the lower the maltreatment rate was in that county. Furthermore, several researchers found that concentrated neighborhood poverty highly correlated with rates of reported and substantiated cases of all types of child abuse and neglect and with the incidence of re-abuse and recurring neglect. The correlation were particularly high for physical abuse and neglect and significant, but lower, for sexual and psychological abuse (Drake & Pandey, 1996; Fryers & Miyoshi, 1994; Jones & McCurdy, 1992; Krugman, Lenherr, Betz, & Fryer, 1986; Tzeng & Schwarzin 1990).

It is suspected that people with low income are over-represented in statistics on child abuse due to their greater use of public health and social service facilities and, consequently, their greater visibility to reporting mechanisms (Gil, 1969; Magnuson, 1983). Some researchers suggest that an individual's perception of how sufficient his or her resources are may be more significant than what his or her resources actual are because an individual's perception is that individual's reality. The perception of not having sufficient resources (e.g., money) may result in stress, which leads to abuse and/or neglect. For example, Lloyd, Cate, and Conger (1983) contend that in nonfunctional families, perceived resources are inadequate to meet family needs and stress and violence are often the consequences. Financially, the family is at its most vulnerable period during its child rearing years (Elmer, 1979) and economic difficulties encountered during that time may result in, or contribute to, abusive behavior (Bybee, 1979; Kempe, 1973; Shanas, 1975; Solomon, 1973; Wright, 1976). Furthermore, Drake and Pandey (1996) suggests that homogeneously poor neighborhoods are also communities characterized by violence and social isolation; and, all of those factors collectively contribute to the incidence of abuse and neglect.

Even though there is a definite correlation between poverty and child abuse and neglect (Besharov & Laumann, 1997; Drakes & Pandey, 1996; Jellinek, Murphy, Poitrast, Quinn, Bishop, & Goshko, 1992), Besharov and Laumann (1997) contend that it is very important to differentiate child maltreatment from poverty and recognize the need for corresponding alternative interventions. Also, literature regarding prevention of child abuse and neglect suggests that it is not accurate or helpful to consider poverty as a cause or sole contributing factor of child abuse and neglect. Parenting is a very difficult task, consisting of a complex mixture of variables which occur not in a vacuum, but in the midst of a myriad of individual, family, societal, and cultural factors (Howze & Kotch, 1984; Kotch, Browne, Ringwalt, Dufort, Ruina, Stewart, & Jung, 1997).

For most parents child rearing is a heavy psychological, social, and financial burden and is replete with child management issues (Reid, Patterson, & Loeber, 1981). Poverty is not a single predictor for the potential risk of abuse or neglect, nor is it a necessary or constant basis for determining abuse potential. Multiple factors contribute to the incidence of child abuse and neglect and occurrences of abuse and neglect are highly complex and convoluted problems (Belsky, 1993; Drake & Pandey, 1996). Factors like family cognitive and behavioral attributes (Silvester, Bentovim, Stratton, & Hanks, 1995), may be more promising and meaningful for considering students' risk status and for understanding abuse and neglect behavior. However, these factors are rather salient and may not be known to educators. Conversely, poverty is an obvious condition and teachers who work in schools that are part of communities plagued with economic problems know the poverty factor and see many of its consequences.

Child Abuse and Neglect

Although exact numbers differ, experts agree that a highly significant number of school-aged children are abused and/or neglected each year. Estimates of the numbers of children who are abused and/or neglected each year range from hundreds of thousands to multiple millions. In 1990 2.7 million children in the United States were reported as being abused, the vast majority of whom were school-aged children (Cappelleri, Eckenrode, & Powers, 1993; Heneson, 1992). According to the Children's Defense Fund (1997), between 1985 and 1995, the number of children reported to be abused and/or neglected increased by 61 percent (up to 3.1 million) and the number of children involved in cases investigated and confirmed increased by 36% (up to 996,000). Furthermore, researchers have reported a 40% to 70% chance of reabuse occurring when children are left in abusive homes and at least a 5% chance of a child being killed after being returned to abusive and/or neglectful parents (Ferleger, Glenwick, Gaines, & Green, 1988; Schmitt & Krugman, 1992). In their study of 206 court cases of severe abuse and neglect, Jellinek, et al. (1992) reported that the abusive parents involved were known by their local departments of social services for an average of two years prior to the court case and were brought to court for the case examined after an average of four official reports were made.

Additionally, some researchers contend that the potential for abuse is universal. That is, the risk for abuse exists in every parent-child relationship and is particularly heightened during child management confrontations (Gil, 1983; Kempe, 1973; Reid, Patterson, & Loeber, 1981). Morris-Bilotti (1991) argues that the status of children in America is worse now than it has been within the last 50 years; with dramatic increases in the incidence of abuse and neglect, the number of children living in poverty, and a myriad of other social ills. Child abuse and neglect has become everyone's problem (Fontana, 1987); it is an issue no one should ignore. Teachers have repeated opportunities to share needed information and suggestions with parents of (a) students who have been abused or neglected who remain in their homes and continue to attend school and (b) students whose experiences do not meet legal definitions of abuse or neglect but experience family problems that include harsh and/or inadequate treatment.

Students who are abused and/or neglected, generally evidence problems with learning and problems with behavior. In fact, child abuse and neglect has been associated with cognitive and behavioral disabilities that require special educational services. Children may acquire disabilities because of abuse and/or neglect or the fact that a child has a disability may make him or her more vulnerable to abuse and neglect (Waldron, 1996; Zirpoli, 1986). Academic failure may result from deficits in attention and/or comprehension skills or from problematic behaviors which disrupt or prohibit instruction. Consequently, classroom behaviors that may be typical for a child who has been abused and/or neglect may not only hinder the achievement of that student, but adversely affect other students as well. In their study of families with 5 to 11 year-old children who had been abused; Manly, Cicchetti, and Barnett (1994) reported that the more long-term, frequent, and severe the abuse or neglect, the more problematic behaviors and less social competence the children exhibited. Furthermore, Perez and Widom (1994) reported that early childhood experiences of abuse and/or neglect not only result in substantial emotional and social disruptions during child development, but also produces long-term intellectual and academic consequences into adulthood. In a study, 413 young adults who had been officially reported as abused and/or neglected were compared with 286 young adults who were not identified as abused or neglected, researchers found a significant difference in IQ and reading ability between the two groups. The childhood victims of abuse and/or neglect evidenced lower levels of IQ and reading ability in young adulthood than the adults who did not have documented childhood histories of abuse and/or neglect (Perez & Widom, 1994).

Researchers have reported that significant relationships exist between child abuse and neglect and K-12 student achievement in the classroom. The results of those investigations have yielded both statistically and educationally significant findings and they have indicated the need for more attention to the associations of child abuse and neglect and student performance. The following are examples of various studies that illustrate research findings regarding various types of abuse (physical abuse, emotional abuse, sexual abuse, and/or neglect). When compared with students who were not abused or neglected, students who were abused or neglected:

1. had lower levels of self-esteem, a factor with well documented links to deficiencies in academic motivation and performance and difficulties with socialization (Kaufman & Cicchetti, 1989; Oates, Peacock, & Forrest, 1984).
2. were most consistently rated by teachers as deficient in academic, social, and emotional functioning (Erickson, Egeland, & Pianta, 1989).
3. scored significantly lower on intelligence tests (Erickson, Egeland, & Pianta, 1989; Perez & Widom, 1994).

4. scored lower on standardized tests in language, reading, and mathematics (Eckenrode, Laird, & Doris, 1993; Perez & Widom, 1994).
5. had lower report card grades in mathematics and reading/English (Dodge-Reyome, 1988; Eckenrode, Laird, & Doris, 1993).
6. were more likely to be recipients of special education services (Vondra, Barnett, & Cicchetti, 1989).
7. were more likely to repeat a grade (Eckenrode, Laird, & Doris, 1993).
8. were more likely to be the subjects of discipline referrals (Eckenrode, Laird, & Doris, 1993).
9. were more aggressive (Egeland & Sroufe, 1981; Hoffman-Plotkin & Twentyman, 1984; Kaufman & Cichetti, 1989; Straker & Jacobson, 1981; Wolfe & Mosk, 1983).
10. were more likely to be suspended from school (Eckenrode, Laird, & Doris, 1993).

Social Support

There are no easy solutions for the problem of child abuse and neglect; but, there are some interventions that have been helpful, including school-based approaches (Tower, 1993). Teachers can influence parenting in positive ways. One way to channel that influence, that is particularly relevant for the prevention of child abuse and neglect, is by becoming an active part of a parent's social support network. Social support involves being helpful and encouraging to someone in a vast number of ways through an interpersonal relationship characterized by caring.

Support from an individual's social network has repeatedly been identified as a buffer against abusive and/or neglectful parent behavior, while the lack of support and/or stressful relationships within an individual's social network have been identified as contributors to abusive parent behavior (Albarracin, Repetto, & Alarracin, 1997; Chan, 1994; Daniel, Hampton, & Newberger, 1983; Kotch, Browne, Ringwalt, Dufort, Ruina, Stewart, & Jung, 1997; Lovell & Hawkins, 1988; Prier & Gulley, 1987). In their study, Gaudin and Pollane (1983) reported that mothers who experienced elevated levels of situational stress but had a strong social support network were less likely to be abusive than mothers who experienced the same levels of situational stress but had inadequate social support. Similarly, as a result of their study, Albarracin, Repetto, & Albarracin (1997) concluded that having a specific source of support was crucial to controlling abusive and neglectful behaviors. Teachers can be a specific source of support for parents; and, they often are supportive in random and informal ways.

Teachers do have an impact on parents during numerous interactions through the school year. Teachers who have developed proficiency in the use of their professional character, knowledge, and skills can interact with parents in socially supportive ways that, in turn, help parents to engage in positive and constructive parenting behaviors. Teachers can informally and/or formally share information with parents and support parents in ways that will result in parents developing and using positive and constructive parenting behaviors.

Recognizing that parenting behavior is determined by numerous variables (Belsky, 1984), it is important to develop a variety of multiple interventions for the prevention of child abuse and neglect and for the development of constructive parenting behaviors. Acronyms associated with parenting (MOM, DAD, FAMILY, and SIBLINGS) help to convey a perspective about teachers' involvement in the prevention of child abuse and neglect. Using the acronym; a justification, a framework, and recommendations for teachers as facilitators of constructive parenting practices are provided. Teacher educators can use this framework in class discussions and lectures to help teachers recognize and use their power to help prevent child abuse and neglect.

Teachers Have . . .

Generally, teachers have contact with the MOMs of their students. Also, teachers have sufficient reasons, avenues, and competencies to interact with the moms in socially supportive ways that can help prevent and/or diminish abusive parent behavior.

MOM

M -<u>MOTIVES</u>. Teachers have multiple motives for helping to prevent child abuse and neglect. Estimates of occurrences of abuse and neglect of school-aged children, academic and social consequences, and absence or insufficiency of responses to official reports demand that teachers respond to the problems of child abuse and neglect in ways that help parents to replace abusive and neglectful behaviors with behaviors conducive to healthy physical, cognitive and emotional child development.

O -<u>OPPORTUNITIES</u>. Teachers have (and can create) numerous opportunities for helping to prevent child abuse and neglect. Individualized educational program (IEP) conferences, "Open House" sessions, parent forums, and other typical and special school events provide repeated opportunities for teachers to talk with parents.

M -<u>MEANS</u>. Teachers have countless means for helping to prevent child abuse and neglect. Knowledge, skills, and insight gained from professional experiences and from courses in child development, behavior management, and instructional strategies can be shared or used with parents.

Teachers Should Also Have . . .

Teachers should reach out to establish relationships with the DADs of their students, since he is likely to have a significant impact on the child's life, present or absent from the home.

DAD

D - <u>DIPLOMACY</u>. Teachers should have diplomatic skills. Teachers need to focus on meeting objectives for working with parents in the interest of the child and avoid personal judgements. They must act as advocates rather than as adversaries.

A - <u>AUTHENTICITY</u>. Teachers should have authentic concerns about parents as people. Teachers need to sincerely care about the parents, not just about the children. If teachers do care about children, they must care about their parents and speak honestly and candidly while also being tactful.

D - <u>DETERMINATION.</u> Teachers should have the determination to do their best for the benefit of children. Teachers need to be persistent. Teachers should expect to repeat information and actions, engage in interventions for prolonged periods, and employ intensive effort.

Teachers Need To Consider . . .

Teachers need to recognize that much of a child's development takes place in the context of the FAMILY. Teachers need to consider multiple family variables when interacting with a child. Teachers need to interact with significant formal and informal family members as well as with the individual student.

FAMILY

F - <u>Family Individualization</u>. Teachers need to consider the fact that families have individual differences. Different families have different structures, beliefs, and needs; they consist of different individuals and they require different approaches for assistance and/or intervention. Each family should be considered collectively and as individual family members.

A - <u>Availability</u>. Teachers need to consider flexible scheduling and multiple modes of communication so they can be available to family members. For example, timing of meetings with family members may only be possible before or after regular school hours and may require flexible scheduling. Teachers also need to consider how emotionally approachable and accessible they wish to be and how they can communicate it to family members.

M - <u>Multiplicity of Elements</u>. Teachers need to consider the fact that a large variety of contributing factors are involved in the prevention of child abuse and neglect. Interventions with families are highly complex issues that involve an undeterminable number of variables and possibilities. Teachers may need to consider several elements simultaneously; but, target one specific element or set of elements and gradually progress to dealing with others. Teachers also need to have their own support systems and resources of persons with expertise in the prevention of child abuse and neglect.

I -<u>Initiative</u>. Teachers need to consider using effective leadership skills in exercising initiative. Teachers need to think about prevention, recognize the importance of taking the initiative in interactions with families and carefully consider the most prudent approach for doing so. Taking the initiative to build functional relationships and offering information and suggestions should be a routine part of the beginning of each school year; family members may be reluctant to seek help, although they may be very glad to receive it.

L -<u>Limitations</u>. Teachers need to consider human, professional, and personal limitations. Teachers must recognize their own individual limitations, the limitations of their role as educators who must not intrude on the role of child community service agencies responsible for addressing issues related to child abuse and neglect, and the limitations of the families they encounter.

Y -<u>Yourself</u>. Teachers need to consider themselves in the prevention of abusive and neglectful behavior. Teachers need to recognize their own potential for being abusive and be certain that they are not abusive. It is essential that teachers model positive and productive interactions with their students and with their students' families.

Teachers Need To Learn About and Discuss . . .

Teachers need to recognize that the SIBLINGS of their students (a) may also be victims of abuse and/or neglect, (b) may be primary or secondary abusers themselves, (c) may be used to assist with the abuse and/or neglect, and/or (d) may be commanded to remain silent in the presence of abuse and/or neglect. Also, siblings may learn abusive and/or neglectful behaviors as acceptable parenting behaviors. In any case, siblings are affected by the occurrences of abuse and neglect within their families and should also be targets of concern. Some topics that teachers need to learn about and be prepared to discuss with parents and/or other family members are listed below. However, teachers need to also be responsive to the specific needs of their students and their students' families; discussing the issues and concerns identified by the individuals involved and based on each opportunity for discussion.

SIBLINGS

S -Stress. Teachers need to be aware of possible manifestations of stress and know some specific strategies for stress reduction and stress management that parents may be receptive to doing.

I -Impact. Teachers need to recognize the impact people in a child's environment have on the child, including the impact of parents, siblings, and significant others. Teachers, also, need to understand the dynamics of direct and indirect impact and be able to discuss their perceptions of a parent's positive or negative impact on a child in a suggestive, rather than directive, manner.

B -Behavior Management. Teachers need to understand principles of behavior management and be able to explain, to others, multiple ways of preventing behavior problems, managing behavior problems, and teaching behavioral competencies. Teachers need to have a repertoire of positive behavior management skills that can be readily modified for use by parents.

L -Listening. Teachers need to practice and be able to teach active listening and reflective practice skills, which involves noticing and interpreting overt and covert cues that represent an assortment of sensory modalities. Consequently, using what is learned to improve performance.

I -Independence. Teachers need to value and teach independence. Teachers need to be able to facilitate the development of self-management skills and the acceptance and exhibition of personal responsibility.

N -<u>Needs</u>. Teachers need to know clearly and concisely stated strategies for conducting personal needs assessments, establishing priorities, and resolving problems of conflicting needs.

G -<u>Goals</u>. Teachers need to know step-by-step guidelines for goal setting, strategic planning, dynamics related to goal attainment.

S -<u>Social Support Network</u>. Teachers need to know how to build social support networks, establish positive support systems with persons with similar Life circumstances, and develop reciprocal relationships among network members.

Evidence of enhanced student achievement as a consequence of educational interventions related to the topics included in the discussion of the SIBLINGS acronym have been noted by several scholars who have reported that they have a positive effect on global academic achievement and also affect specific elements related to academic achievement: (a) school attendance rates, (b) motivation for learning, (c) educational expectations, (d) personal responsibility for learning, (e) in-school and out-of-school conduct, and (f) positive peer influence regarding academics and behavior (Aldridge, 1993; Coil, 1994; Costa, 1985; Gootman, 1993; Helge, 1989; Kaplan, 1991; Kreidler, 1984; Lengel, 1989; Marsh, 1984; Purkey, 1970; Wirth, 1977).

Teacher educators can use individualized professional growth plans to have teachers develop and practice skills identified in the acronym outline.

Conclusion

Statistics that estimate the number of school-aged children who are abused and/or neglected strongly suggest that all teachers will, at some time during their professional careers, have students who are abused and/or neglected. The fact that teachers are mandated reporters of suspicions of child abuse and neglect has not resulted in its decline; and, limiting teachers' role to reporting does not make use of a greatly needed and greatly capable resource. Teacher educators can be most instrumental in helping teachers develop and use competencies that can help prevent child abuse and neglect.

References

Albarracin, D., Repetto, M. J., & Albarracin, M. (1997). Social support in child abuse and neglect: Support functions, sources, and contexts. Child Abuse & Neglect, 21, 607-615.

Aldridge, J. (1993). Self-esteem: Loving yourself at every age. Birmingham, AL: Doxa Books.

Belsky, J. (1984). The determinants of parenting: A process model. Child Development, 55, 83-96.

Belsky, J. (1993). Etiology of child maltreatment: A developmental analysis. Psychological Bulletin, 114(3), 413-434.

Besharov, D. J., & Laumann, L. A. (1997). Don't call it child abuse if it's really poverty. Journal of Children and Poverty, 3, 5-36.

Bybee, R. (1979). Violence toward youth: A new perspective. Journal of Social Issues, 35, 1-13.

Cappelleri, J. C., Eckenrode, J., & Powers, J. L. (1993). The epidemiology of child abuse: Findings from the second national incidence and prevalence study of child abuse and neglect. American Journal of Public Health, 83, 1622-1624.

Chan, Y. C. (1994). Parenting stress and social support of mothers who physically abuse their children in Hong Kong. Child Abuse & Neglect, 18, 261-269.

Children Defense Fund. (1997). The state of America's children. Washington, DC: Children's Defense Fund.

Coil, C. (1994). Becoming an achiever. (K. Balsamo, Ed.). Beavercreek, OH: Pieces of Learning.

Costa, A. L. (Ed.). (1985). Developing minds. Alexandria, VA: Association for Supervision and Curriculum Development.

Daniel, J. H., Hampton, R. L., & Newberger, E. H. (1983). Child abuse and accidents in Black families: A controlled comparative study. American Journal of Orthopsychiatry, 53, 645-653.

Dodge-Reyome, N. (1988). An investigation of the school performance of sexually abused and neglected children. Unpublished doctoral dissertation, Cornell University.

Drake, B., & Pandey, S. (1996). Understanding the relationship between neighborhood poverty and specific types of child maltreatment. Child Abuse & Neglect, 20, 1003-1018.

Eckenrode, J., Laird, M., & Doris, J. (1993). School performance and disciplinary problems among abused and neglected children. Developmental Psychology, 29, 53-62.

Egeland, B., & Sroufe, L. A. (1981). Attachment and early maltreatment. Child Development, 52, 44-52.

Elmer, E. (1979). Child abuse and family stress. Journal of Social Issues, 35(2), 60-71.

Erickson, M. F., Egeland, B., & Pianta, R. (1989). The effects of maltreatment on the development of young children. In D. Cicchetti & V. Carlson (Eds.), Child maltreatment: Theory and research on the causes and consequences of child abuse and neglect (pp. 647-684). Cambridge, England: Cambridge University Press.

Ferleger, N., Glenwick, D. S., Gaines, R. W., & Green, A. H. (1988). Identifying correlates of reabuse in maltreating parents. Child Abuse & Neglect, 12, 41-49.

Fontana, V. J. (1973). The diagnosis of the maltreatment syndrome in children. Pediatrics, 51, 780-782.

Fryer, G. E., Miyoshi, T. J. (1994). A survival analysis of the revictimization of children: The case of Colorado. Child Abuse & Neglect, 18, 1063-1071.

Garbarino, J., & Sherman, D. (1980). High-risk neighborhoods and high-risk families: The human ecology of child maltreatment. Child Development, 51, 188-198.

Gaudin, J. M., & Pollane, L. (1983). Social networks, stress and child abuse. Children and Youth Services Review, 5, 91-102.

Gil, D. (1969). What schools can do about child abuse. American Education, 5, 2-4.

Gil, D. (1983). The United States versus child abuse. Journal of Clinical Child Psychology, 12, 300-306.

Gootman, M. E. (1993). Reaching and teaching abused children. Childhood Education 70(1), 15-19.

Helge, D. (1989). Report of pilot project regarding strategies for enhancing self-esteem of at-risk students. Bellingham, WA: Western Washington University, National Rural and Small Schools Consortium.

Heneson, L. (1992). The Secretary's initiative on child abuse and neglect. Children Today, 21(2), 4-7.

Hoffman-Plotkin, D., & Twentyman, C. (1984). A multimodal assessment of behavioral and cognitive deficits in abused and neglected preschoolers. Child Development, 55, 794-802.

Howze, D. C., & Kotch, J. B. (1984). Disentangling life events, stress and social support: Implications for the primary prevention of child abuse and neglect. Child Abuse & Neglect, 8, 401-409.

Jellinek, M. S., Murphy, J. M., Poitrast, F., Quinn, D., Bishop, S. J., & Goshko, M. (1992). Serious child maltreatment in Massachusetts: The course of 206 children through the courts. Child Abuse & Neglect, 16, 179-185.

Jones, E. D., & McCurdy, K. (1992). The links between types of maltreatment and demographic characteristics of children. Child Abuse & Neglect, 16, 201-215.

Kaplan, J. S. (1991). Beyond behavior modification (2nd ed.). Austin, TX: Pro-Ed.

Kaufman, J., & Cicchetti, D. (1989). Effects of maltreatment on school-age children's socioemotional development: Assessment in a day-camp setting. Developmental Psychology, 25, 516-524.

Kempe, C. (1973). A practical approach to the protection of the abused child and rehabilitation of the abusing parent. Pediatrics, 51, 804-812.

Kotch, J. B., Browne, D. C., Ringwalt, C. L., Dufort, V., Ruina, E., Stewart, P. W., & Jung, J. (1997). Stress, social support, and substantiated maltreatment in the second and third years of life. Child Abuse & Neglect, 21, 1025-1037.

Kreidler, W. J. (1984). Creative conflict resolution. Glenview, IL: Good Year.

Krugman, R., Lenherr, M., Betz, L., & Fryer, G. (1986). The relationship between unemployment and physical abuse of children. Child Abuse & Neglect, 10, 415-418.

Lengel, A. (1989). Mentee/mentor: Someone in my corner. Gifted Child Today 12(1), 27-29.

Letourneau, C. (1981). Empathy and stress: How they affect parental aggression. Social Work, 26, 383-389.

Lovell, M. L., & Hawkins, J. D. (1988). An evaluation of a group intervention to increase the personal social networks of abusive mothers. Children and Youth Services Review, 10, 175-188.

Lloyd, S. A., Cate, R. M., & Conger, J. (1983). Family violence and service providers: Implications for training. Social Casework, 64, 431-435.

Magnuson, E. (1983, September). Child abuse: The ultimate betrayal. Time, pp. 20-22.

Manly, J. T., Cicchetti, D., & Barnett, D. (1994). The impact of subtype, frequency, chronicity, and severity of child maltreatment on social competence and behavior problems. Development and Psychopathology, 6, 121-143.

Marsh, H. W. (1984). Relations among dimensions of self-attribution, dimensions of self-concept and academic achievement. Journal of Educational Psychology, 76, 1291-1308.

McCurdy, K., & Daro, D. (1994). Child maltreatment: A national survey of reports and fatalities. Journal of Interpersonal Violence, 9, 75-94.

Morris-Bilotti, S. (1991). The plight of America's children: A plea for entitlement. Springfield, IL: Illinois State Department of Children and Family Services.

Oates, R. K., Peacock, A., & Forrest, D. (1984). Development in children following abuse and nonorganic failure to thrive. American Journal of Disorders in Children, 138, 764-767.

Perez, C. M., Widom, C. S. (1994). Childhood victimization and long-term intellectual and academic outcomes. Child Abuse & Neglect, 18, 617-633.

Prier, R. E., & Gulley, M. I. (1987). A comparison of rates of child abuse in U. S. Army families stationed in Europe and in the United States. Military Medicine, 152, 437-440.

Purkey, W. W. (1970). Self-concept and school achievement. Englewood Cliffs, NJ: Prentice Hall.

Reid, J. B., Patterson, G. R., & Loeber, R. (1981). The abused child: Victim, instigator, or innocent bystander? Nebraska symposium on motivation: Response, structure, and organization (pp. 47-68). Lincoln, N?: University of Nebraska.

Schmitt, B., Krugman, R. (1992). Abuse and neglect of children. In R. Behrman & R. Kliegman (Eds.), Nelson textbook of pediatrics (14th ed.). (pp 78-83). Philadelphia, PA: Saunders.

Shanas, B. (1975). Child abuse: A killer teachers can help to control. Phi Delta Kappan, 56, 479-482.

Silvester, J., Bentovim, A., Stratton, P., & Hanks, H. G. I. (1995). Using spoken attributions to classify abusive families. Child Abuse & Neglect, 19, 1221-1232.

Solomon, T. (1973). History and demography of child abuse. Pediatrics, 51, 773-776.

Spearly, J. L., & Lauderdale, M. (1983). Community characteristics and ethnicity in the prediction of child maltreatment rates. Child Abuse & Neglect, 7, 91-105.

Straker, G., & Jacobson, R. S. (1981). Aggression, emotional maladjustment, and empathy in the abused child. Developmental Psychology, 17, 762-765.

Tower, C. C. (1993). Understanding child abuse and neglect (2nd ed.).Boston: Allyn and Bacon.

Tzeng, O., & Schwarzin, H. (1990). Gender and race differences in child sexual abuse correlates. International Journal of Intercultural Relations, 14, 135-161.

United States Department of Health, Education, & Welfare. (1977). National analysis of official child abuse and neglect reporting (DHEW Publication No. OHDS 79-30232). Washington, DC: U. S. Government Printing Office.

Vondra, J., Barnett, D., & Cicchetti, D. (1989). Perceived and actual competence among maltreated and comparison school children. Development and Psychopathology, 1, 237-255.

Waldron, N. L. (1996). Child abuse and disability: The school's role in prevention and intervention. Preventing School Failure, 40, 164-168.

Webster-Stratton, C. (1985). Comparison of abusive and nonabusive families with conduct-disordered children. American Journal of Orthopsychiatry, 55, 59-69.

Wirth, S. (1977). Effects of a multifaceted reading program on self-concept. Elementary School Guidance & Counseling, 12, 33-39.

Wolfe, D., & Mosk, M. D. (1983). Behavioral comparisons of children from abusive and distressed families. Journal of Consulting and Clinical Psychology, 15, 702-708.

Wright, L. (1976). The "sick but slick" syndrome as a personality component of parents of battered children. Journal of Clinical Psychology, 32, 41-45.

Zirpoli, T. J. (1986). Child abuse and children with handicaps. Remedial and Special Education, 7(2), 39-48.

Chapter Three

MAKING CONNECTIONS IN SCIENC AND MATHEMATICS A MEANS TO MOTIVATE MINORITY STUDENTS

Shelbie M. Anderson, Associate Professor
University of Arkansas at Pine Bluff

African American, Hispanic/Latino, Native American, and other culturally diverse individuals comprise approximately 18% of the United States population, but only 2.2% of our technical work force. The numbers of culturally diverse students enrolled in mathematics, science, computer science, and computer engineering studies remain low, despite the removal of many social and legal barriers to the full participation of these students in science careers... Many high ability and culturally or linguistically diverse students and many of those with high potential face not only educational but also economic barriers in their pursuit of training for high-tech jobs (
Barba, p.

Science and mathematics are two of the most important subject areas taught in our schools, however, these two subject areas seem to be out of reach to certain minority groups, namely, Blacks, Hispanics, and Native Americans. Although research show that minority students are underachievers in mathematics and science, all children can learn both subjects if taught properly and with meaning.

The importance of science and mathematics cannot not be overstated because it affects the everyday lives of all people. There are two important reasons for teaching science and mathematics in our schools. First, science and mathematics are everyday experiences. As individuals, especially in the industrialized countries of the world, and indirectly in the non-industrialized countries of the world, we experience science and mathematics from the moment we awaken each day to the moment we fall asleep, and even then, science and mathematics are constantly in action while we sleep. Secondly, most of the career opportunities and career choices an individual makes are dependent on a person's knowledge of science and mathematics. The jobs that pay the most are the ones that are heavily indoctrinated in science and mathematics.

It is possible to teach all children mathematics regardless of their cultural heritage. All children bring to school some type of experiential background. This background becomes the essence from which we capitalize on to teach them mathematics and science.

Children differ in many ways. Most minority children have very unique backgrounds due to their cultural heritage and/or socioeconomic status. Many times teachers fail to capture the richness of each child's experiential background. In order to capitalize on the experiential richness that each child brings to the classroom, teachers must understand the cultural heritage that minority children possess. This heritage becomes the foundation that we build on to motivate and teach children mathematics and science.

In order to meet the needs of culturally different children, teachers must teach mathematics and science to minority to children so as to make them culturally relevant. Culturally relevant mathematics or culturally relevant science are new terms in the vocabulary of mathematics and science education. The terms indicates an awareness on the part of educators that all subjects, including mathematics and science, exist within a cultural environment that must not be ignored (Hatfield, et al, p. 77).

Most minority children have very unique backgrounds due to their cultural heritage and/or socioeconomic status. Many times teachers fail to capture the richness of each child's experiential background. In order to capitalize on the experiential richness that each child brings to the classroom, teachers must understand the cultural heritage that minority children possess. This heritage becomes the foundation that we build on to motivate and teach children mathematics.

It is so easy for teachers to become frustrated with children who are different. However, they must believe that all children can learn and this includes minority children. If teachers do not believe that children can learn mathematics and science, they have already defeated the cause and wasted their efforts to motivate and teach mathematics and science to children.

This chapter will not focus on the career opportunities that are dependent on science and mathematics, however, it will pursue the subjects with the intention of helping educators to challenge and motivate children to learn and comprehend mathematics and science in the context of connecting the two subjects to culturally relevant experiences. If educators are successful in motivating children to learn mathematics and science through interesting and meaningful activities, then they will be able to master the two content areas so as to enable them to pursue careers in highly technical occupations.

The chapter will be divided into three categories:

- Principles and Connections for Teaching Science Meaningfully to Minority Students With Suggestions for Reinforcement at School and at Home
- Principles and Connections for Teaching Mathematics Meaningfully and Suggestions for Reinforcement at School and at Home
- Integrating Science and Mathematics to Form Meaningful Contexts

Principles and Connections for Teaching Science Meaningfully to Minority Students

It is important to establish in the classroom an awareness of the fact that science surrounds us. Therefore, it is necessary to make the connections between children's natural curiosity and scientific endeavors. Investigation is an integral part of scientific inquiry. Through investigations, children can be problem posers and problem solvers. Scientific knowledge, in all its applications, permits humans to control the environment in which they exist. It is by doing (or hands-on activities) that children learn about science in meaningful contexts. It is the teachers responsibility to provide hands-on activities as a means of challenging all students to continue their curiosity and to become investigators of phenomena that arouse their curiosity in the safe environment of the classroom. It is also important that teachers utilize problem solving as the core of their scientific instructional program.

Dolby, Beichner, and Raimondi (1999) identified six principles of teaching elementary school science that are relevant when teaching minority students science. They are:

- Children Can Be Problem Posers and Investigators
- The Teacher's Role Is as a Guide
- Nature Is the Authority
- There are No Right or Wrong Answers
- Hands-On/Minds-on Experience is a Must
- Attitude Building is Important.

The way that science is taught today is very different from that which was taught in the past. In today's schools, students are actively involved in the learning process. They are presented with hands-on/minds-on activities in which they critically examine their surroundings and communicate their findings to each other as a means of comparing and assessing the information they have discovered.

According to Dolby and et al., teachers provide a learning environment for their students. That's all they can do. They can't force facts into children heads, although they can motivate the students to study. They can't build the synopses in a student's brain that relate two concepts, but they can show the student how the ideas go together. They shouldn't be the final authority on any specific scientific fact. This is where teachers have trouble

(p. 30).

♦ Children Can Be Problem Posers and Investigators

Scientific knowledge, in all its applications, permits humans to control the environment in which they exist. It is by doing science, rather than hearing about science, or reading about science that children learn about science in a meaningful contest. Minority children by their very experiences, are hands-on learners. Therefore, teachers should utilize problem solving as the core of the instructional process in science.

Suggestions for Teachers

Use a constructivist approach to teaching. Connect new knowledge to prior experiences and understandings minority students have. Take time to help students focus on prior experiences they may have had to make the necessary connections. (This will be difficult to do, if the teacher has not developed a multicultural prospective and is not knowledgeable about the cultural nuances of a particular cultural group).

Provide a wide variety of hands-on experiences that will enable minority students to develop a knowledge base for what is being taught if one is not available.

Utilize probing questions that will elicit responses from students about a scientific phenomena.

Suggestions for Parents

Set aside a special time to spend with your child in which you can take walks through the neighborhood, park, or on a nature trail. Take time to talk with your child.

Ask your child "what," "why," and "how" types of questions about what he sees and hears while your are taking a walk with the child.

At least once a week, sit and look at the Discovery Channel with your child. Have your child explain the reason why some animals behave as they do and/or why they live the way they do.

There Are No Right or Wrong Answers, Only Careful Observations

Because of the experiential bases of finding answers to questions, there are no simple right or wrong answers. The results of an experiment is dependent on what nature did during the experiment and that is what should have, in fact must have happened. At times the question originally posed may not be answered because of poor measurement techniques or an incomplete gathering of data. The key to teaching children is to teach them to be careful and thorough in their investigations.

Suggestions for Teachers

Avoid the authoritarian approach to teaching. Teachers do not know or have all the answers to questions students may pose. Allow the students to explore, experiment, and to discover.

Suggestions for Parents

When talking with your child, remember B a situation may have more than one prospective or point of view. Encourage your child to rationalize his/her answer to see if there may be another **possible answer. Allow your child the opportunity to explain his/her answer to you.**

Hands-On/Mind-On Experience Is a Must

Elementary school age children understand concrete ideas easier than they grasp abstract ideas. It is the teacher's responsibility to provide a stimulating environment for the children to explore. Include a variety of hands-on experiments in your teaching plan. Ask the children probing questions as they perform their experiment. Probing questions will enable the students to do critical thinking.

Suggestions for Teachers

In addition to those strategies mentioned above, remember, most minority children have had a wealth of hands-on experiences during play. Challenge them with a variety of experiments that explore a concept they are manipulating. Ask lead questions to get them to think about the experiment and what they have discovered and why the experiment worked the way it did. Teach them how to assess their learning.

Suggestions to Parents

Plant a plant, or a garden, with your child. Watch the garden grow. Observe the plant, or garden, as it grows. Discuss with the child the reason why the plant(s) is/are healthy, or unhealthy. If the plant appears to be unhealthy, ask your child if he/she can think of a reason why the plants seem sick. Ask your child probing questions about the plant/garden.

Attitude Building Is Important

In order to prevent students from having a negative attitude about science, it is the teacher's responsibility to work hard during the formative years to show the children the wonders of science and scientific endeavor. Science is an exciting and fascinating subject that will motivate children to think, and to inquire as to why the teacher must also show enthusiasm for the subject while working with children. If the teacher is not excited about teaching and does not portray her excitement to her students, her negativism will be modeled by the students. Enthusiasm generates enthusiasm. Challenging activities always inspire children to want to learn. As a means of motivating minority children to participate actively in science and to learn, the teacher must plan hands-on activities.

Suggestions for Teachers

Connect the importance for learning science to the social utility for science. Also relate science to different careers that have a scientific foundation. Present a positive, enthusiastical attitude while teaching science. Demonstrate to students that you believe that science is worthwhile.

Suggestions for Parents

Discuss with your child the importance of science. Also discuss career opportunities related to science. Encourage your child to begin thinking about what he/she wants to be when they grow up. Talk with your child about careers in science

Principles and Connections for Teaching Mathematics Meaningfully to Minority Students

In order to be effective teachers of mathematics, it is important that teachers are cognizant about how children learn mathematics. Research has demonstrated the importance of the process of building bridges from the concrete to the symbolic and helping children cross them in the heart of good teaching, and it is a continual challenge. The following principles for teaching mathematics in the elementary school are based on a blend of research, teaching experience, and thinking about how children learn mathematics (Reys, Suydam, Lindquist, and Smith (1998).

Reys and et al. have identified eleven principles that apply to teaching mathematics in the elementary school. These principles are briefly discussed with suggestions given for teachers and parents in the following paragraphs.

Actively Involve Students

Active involvement will encourage students to make sense out of what they are doing and thereby develop a greater understanding of mathematics. When children are involved in using models, making decisions, and thinking mathematically, rather than methodically applying formulas, learning is more meaningful. Active involvement may provide for physical activity but always demands mental activity. It takes many forms, including interaction of children and teachers, hands-on experience with manipulatives, and use of special learning materials such as textbooks or technology. One of the daily challenges of teaching is to provide experiences that will encourage, promote, and reward active involvement. Active involvement is the cornerstone on which students construct their own mathematical meaning.

Suggestions for Teachers

It is the teacher's role to include a variety of manipulative materials in their daily plans so as to enable students to make sense out of mathematics. The manipulatives should relate to the concept being taught.

Suggestions for Parents

There are a number of situations found in the home that parents can use to help their child understand mathematical concept. An empty egg carton can be use to teach children how many items make up a dozen. Buttons can be counted and classified. Straws can be used to demonstrate addition and subtraction operations by counting out a number of straws to represent a number and adding additional straws to represent another number in order to find the total number of straws in the two groups. The same can be true with subtraction. A number of straws can be grouped together in which a certain number of straws can be taken from that group of straws to find the difference.

Parents can consult the classroom teacher for suggestions on activities using manipulatives in the home as a reinforcement of what the child is learning at home.

Learning Is Developmental

Mathematics topics should be appropriate for the developmental level of children, and presented and in enjoyable and interesting ways that challenge children's intellectual development. The teacher's role is to establish a rich environment to and explore mathematics at an appropriate developmental level. The teacher should also provide the necessary direction to help children recognize relationships, make connections, and talk about mathematics. It takes time to extract mathematics from real life experiences and concrete materials. This effort helps to develop a lasting facility, not only to think mathematically but also to think mathematically. It takes time to extract mathematics from real life experiences and concrete materials. This effort helps develop a lasting facility not only to talk about mathematics but also to think mathematically (p. 23).

Suggestions for Teachers

It is the teacher's role to emphasize mathematical concepts and relationships in order to develop understandings and to relate mathematical knowledge to the learning of skills by establishing relationships between the conceptual and procedural aspects of a task.

Suggestions for Parents

Since learning is developmental, parents should not push their children to learn mathematics beyond their readiness level. To attempt to surpass what is being taught in school may create mathematics anxiety thus making the child dislike mathematics.

♦ **Build On Previous Learning**

Instructional planning must consider the prerequisites needed for success on the current lesson, and the teacher must check to see if students have them. Detecting these weaknesses early and quickly allows the inclusion of reviews, so that later lesson development is not hampered by students's lack of prerequisites.

Suggestions for Teachers

Before teaching any lesson, it is necessary to see if the children are ready for the new learning. This may be done by initiating an oral review or a written pretest. If the students do not have the necessary prerequisite skills, the teacher needs to do some re-teaching as a means of ascertaining that the students will have the necessary skills for the new experience.

Suggestions for Parents

Parents have the opportunity to look inside their child's notebook to see what he/she did at school. If the student is having difficulty understanding a concept, the parents could proceed to help the child, if they feel comfortable doing so, or call the homework HELP Line if there is such a program in the community.

Parents should be very supportive and patient with the child and try not to push the child too hard when helping the child with homework so as not to create any mathophobia, or math anxiety, in the child.

Communication Is Integral

Utilizing models, manipulatives, and real-world examples provide many opportunities for stimulating thinking, talking, and listening. Teachers should provide students with many opportunities to use language to communicate their mathematical ideas. Opportunities to explain, conjecture, and defend one's ideas orally and in writing can stimulate a deeper understanding of concepts and principles. Communication is a vital part of mathematical thinking. Teachers can help students develop awareness of their best learning techniques by asking questions, conducting discussions, and reward children's thinking (Riedesel and et al.).

Suggestions for Teachers

Help students develop awareness of their best learning techniques by asking questions and conducting discussions. Explain to the students that when they give explanations, think aloud, and react to classmates's thinking, that they are participating in essential elements of the learning process. Allow students to ask questions of each other. Ask probing questions to enable your students to think critically. Encourage students to share their thinking with the class.

Suggestions to Parents

Questions are a vital element in the learning process. Ask your child to explain how he or she got the answer to a problem. When checking out the specials at supermarkets, ask your child to tell you which items would be the best buy. When your are following a recipe when baking or cooking, let your child participate by asking him or her questions such as How much sugar would I need if I doubled the recipe? or What would happen if I used twice as much milk as the recipe calls for? By asking such questions, you will stimulate your child's thinking about relationships and will also help your child to make meaningful connections about mathematics.

Good Questions Facilitate Learning

Questions are a vital element of the learning process. Teachers need to when to ask a question and what kinds of questions to ask. They need to know when to answer a question and when to ask a follow-up question that will facilitate the answering of a previous question. Teachers can help students develop awareness of their best learning techniques by asking questions, conducting discussions, and rewarding children's thinking efforts (Riedesel and et al.).

Suggestions for Teachers

(See suggestions above).

Suggestions for Parents

(See suggestions above)

Manipulatives Aid Learning

Manipulative materials aid children in understanding the conceptual structure of mathematics. Because mathematics by its own nature is an abstract entity, utilizing manipulative materials enables children to make sense out of mathematics. Utilize a variety of manipulative materials so that children will not connect an operation with just one set of manipulatives but can see how problems are solved with a variety of manipulative materials.

Suggestions for Teachers

Once you have used manipulative material to introduce a concept, do not put the manipulatives back in the closet. Always leave the material out so that if a student needs to use the manipulatives, they will be available. Do not discourage a student from using the manipulatives. Students who use manipulatives will wean themselves once they understand the structure of the concept. Manipulatives are also used to solve problems in high school.

Suggestions for Parents

There are many things in your home that you can use to help your child make sense out of mathematics. The egg carton is a good source to help your child think mathematically. Parents can ask their child a question such as: There are twelve eggs in a carton. If I cook three eggs, how many eggs are left in the carton? Allow your child to help you when you are measuring ingredients when cooking. Teach your child what 1/3 of a cup means, etc. Look around the house for every opportunity you can find that your can involve your child in thinking mathematically.

Metacognition Affects Learning

How a learner perceives his ability to do mathematics greatly effect how he or she performs in mathematics. It is the teacher's responsibility to help the student assess his or her strengths and/or weaknesses in mathematics. When students are working on a mathematics problem, ask the students questions that will enable them to stop and think about the process that they are using and why they used the process. Such questions as: "How did you arrive at your answer?", "What did you do when you see an unfamiliar problem?", "Is there another way to get the answer?", "What kind of error do you usually make when you work problems such as this?" "What kind of problems are you best at?" help students to reflect back over the procedures they used in getting an answer. By asking such questions, students will become aware of their strengths, weaknesses, and typical behaviors and of the repertoire of procedures they can use to solve problems. The way a student perceives himself or herself as a learner and how a student controls and adjust his/her behavior has implication for the teacher when making assignments. If a student perceives an assignment as being "too easy," the student may feel unchallenged and may become bored and lose interest in mathematics. In the meantime, the same may be true for students who view an assignment as being "too difficult," and refuse to attempt the assignment. Assignments must be viewed by minority students as Ado-able," i.e., assignments that are within their ability that requires a moderate amount of effort to accomplish. Each minority student must feel that he/she is capable of doing the assignment successfully.

Suggestions for Teachers

According to Reys, Suydam, and Lindquist (1998) encouraging students to think about their thinking is an important ingredient of mathematics learning. They made several suggestions of things teachers can do to help students develop this metacognitive awareness. They suggested that:

Make explicit how they themselves work when solving problems. Explain to the students **why you** did what you did, why you knew not to information that is not relevant to the solution to the problem, if such information is given in the problem, and why you estimated the answer to the problem. Teachers inquire about such information from students, but such information as to why teachers do certain things is not always made known to the students.

Point out to students various aspects of problem solving, such as the following:

Some problems take a long time to solve.

You don't have to solve problems the way the teacher does.

3. Students should also be encouraged to become more aware of metcognition and the need to think about their mathematical thinking. For example, teachers might ask students to discuss the following:

What mathematics problems do you like best? Tell why.

What mathematics problems are most difficult?

What can you do to improve as a solver of these problems?

What do you do when you find a mathematics problem that you don't how to do?

Teacher Attitudes Are Vital

Students's attitudes toward mathematics is often influenced by the teacher's attitude and actions as he/she teaches the subject. If a teacher is enthusiastic and enjoys teaching mathematics, students will respond positively toward mathematics.

Suggestions for Teachers

Always approach your teaching of mathematics with a positive attitude. Show enthusiasm about mathematics while teaching.

Experiences Influence Anxiety

Mathophobia, or mathematics anxiety is a fear of mathematics and may result from the way mathematics is perceived at home among family members and/or as a result of practices exhibited by the teacher in the classroom. Hatfield Edwards, and Bitter (1993) and Kennedy Tipps (1994) identified some reasons given for mathematics anxiety. The reasons given in their textbooks included: overemphasis on one correct answer, use of ambiguous vocabulary, intolerance for unusual ways to solve problems, authoritarian teaching, and pressure from timed tests.

Suggestions for Teachers

To reduce mathematics anxiety, project enthusiasm for mathematics while teaching, utilize cooperative learning groups so that students will have a support group while learning strategies for solving mathematical problems, have and use a variety of manipulative materials, and believe in the students ability to perform in mathematics.

Gender Aptitudes are Equal

Often there exist gender inequities related to the study of mathematics in our society. These inequities may be the result of parent expectations, i.e., boys are the ones who need mathematics, career recommendations by school counselors, i.e., many times girls are discouraged from pursuing careers with mathematical emphasis, or teachers's attitudes towards gender, i.e., mathematics is a boys's subject, thus teachers encourage boys to pursue mathematics subjects and to excel in mathematics.

Suggestions for Teachers

Encourage and challenge girls to excel in mathematics by having them to research female mathematicians, researching various career with mathematics emphasis, and equally calling on them in class.

Suggestions for Parents

Encourage your daughters to excel in mathematics. Discuss with them the many careers that have a mathematics foundation.

Retention Can Improve

Retention is a very important goal in mathematics education. Retention refers to the amount of knowledge kept, skills maintained, or problem solving behavior consistently exhibited by students. Retention is an important goal in mathematics education. Instructional efforts mus recognize the importance of retention and try to maximize it. Three Ways to improve retention (Rey, et al.):

Suggestions for Teachers

Meaningful learning is the best way to shore up retention. All phases of mathematics that have been developed with meaning and learned with understanding are retained longer.

Connections help children see how mathematical ideas are related. Mathematical topics must be taught in isolation as discrete topics, but they must be developed in conjunction with problem solving and applications that cut across several areas whenever possible.

Periodic reviews of selected key ideas contribute substantially to the quantity of mathematics retained. A regular maintenance program removes rustiness and provides important reinforcement and refreshers that improve immediate performance.

Integrating Science and Mathematics to Form Meaningful Contexts

The National Science Education Program Standard C recommends that the science program should be coordinated with mathematics program to enhance student use and understanding of mathematics in the study of science and to improve student understanding of mathematics (p. 214). According to Standard C, if teachers of mathematics use scientific examples and methods, understanding in both disciplines will be enhanced.

Many teachers use an integrated mathematics/science approach to instruction. This approach to teaching science and mathematics enables teachers to stress the real world applications of the study of mathematics and science. An integrated approach to teaching science and mathematics enables minority students to make connections between the two subject in a meaningful way. They are able to see the scientific and social utility, thus making science and mathematics much more interesting.

By utilizing an integrated unit approach for teaching science and mathematics, teachers can plan their units around the interest of the students in the class, they increase the interest and motivation of their students. When teachers use an integrated approach toward teaching science and mathematics, they are also able to incorporate career awareness in their instruction, which would be another motivational way to emphasize the importance of the two subjects.

References

Barba, Robertta H. (1998). Science in the multicultural classroom: A guide to teaching and Learning (2nd edition). Boston, MA: Allyn and Bacon.

Esler, William K. and Esler, Mary K. (1996). Teaching elementary science (7th edition). Boston, MA: Wadsworth Publishing Company.

Kennedy, Leonard and Tipps, Steve (1994). Guiding children=s learning of mathematics (7th edition). Belmont, CA: Wadsworth Publishing Company.

National Research Council (1996). National Science Education Standards. Washington, D.C.: National Academy Press.

Reys, Robert et al. (1998). Helping children learn mathematics (5th edition). Boston, MA: Allyn and Bacon.

Riedesel, C. Alan and Schwartz, James E. (1999). Essentials of Elementary Mathematics (2nd Edition. Boston, MA: Allyn and Bacon.

Chapter 4

**The Implications of Utilizing Eurocentric Constructs
In theEducation of Poor African American School Children.**

Michael E. Orok, Ph.D.
Albnay State University

Teresa Merriweather-Orok, Ph.D.
Albany State University

There is tremendous concern about the nature of education available to minority children in the United States. Some researchers see the parent-school dichotomy as being the prevailing contributing factor that drives how minorities learn and receive instructions in school. Often, the teacher and the previously designed system of education is left out of the analytical loop. (Brown, 1986) recognized this problem earlier on when he wrote that,

> *A historically, public education has been and continues to be controlled by members of the dominant culture in our society. It is a system whose major benefits accrue to white middle- class Americans. As such, the delivery of instructional services to and the learning outcomes for minority students reflect the many inequities the system continues to inflict upon them. (p.1).*

It is against this contextual backdrop that a discussion about the differentiated methods and techniques of instructio al delivery is carried out. In fact, no discourse about the ability of minorities to learn ought to be carried out without engaging in an informed dialogue about the disparity in the United States system of education and its impact on the learning outcome of minority groups. An essential goal in America is the development of a literate society. This goal however, cannot be achieved without making adjustments in the educational setting, especially for children who are often termed the disadvantaged (William and Lehrer,1972). Members of the education profession must be clear about the goal and objectives that they seek to achieve within the prevailing ideological environment (Fulton, 1972). In fact, how those goals are pursued condition our perceptions of what should become a part of the learning process. Many times, our attempt to evade issues that have ethnocentric ramifications and importance limits our view of what education ought to be, hence what makes a child educated

The Poor African American School-Age Child

A majority of ethnic minorities live in central cities, therefore urban schools are increasingly made up of minority students, many of who are African Americans. The values of which the children are exposed to at home are different from those at school. Family life experiences for the poor African American child is dominated by such issues as absentee fathers, low income, step families, extended families and poor housing (Nelson-LeGall, 1994). LeGall further admits that often, the home environment and experiences of inner city teachers and school administrators are distinctly different from those of the children under their care. In the inner cities, there is high unemployment rate, a lack of safe and reliable transportation and the management of limited resources by poor families become a major feat. As a result of the poor, deplorable and often devastating conditions, children grow up with unique experiences, that are theoretically opposed to what the larger society considers to be positive reinforces. Although these children grow up in these unfulfilled environments, they are expected to identify with and accept the strategies, examples, symbols and methods of teaching used by teachers who for the most part have never experienced their pain. This presents a level of cultural incompatibility that aside from issues of poverty, has not been introduced into the curriculum of inner city schools.

The experiences of African-American children in American schools are different from one group to the next (Phenice and et al.,1986, and Tharp, 1989). For example, in the <u>Harvard Educational Review</u> in 1986 (Phenice et. al., 1986) posit that certain Asian groups such as Japanese, Korean, and some South East Asian who are considered immigrant groups succeed in school at the same level as most middle class white children because they have not been repeatedly exposed to any negative symbols or ethnic discrimination. On the other hand, Ogbu, (1978,1986) contends that ethnic groups, especially those whose members who came from a caste system, as described by Ogbu, do not perform well in American schools. This group consists of African Americans , Puerto Ricans, Mexican Americans and Native Americans. Phenice follows this same line of argument and points out that:

> A distinctive views of education by ethnic groups may explain why certain groups respond differently to schooling. Emphasis on ethnicity in school success, however should not obscure other processes of differentiation that have nothing to do with values and much to do with the discrimination and exclusion and education which characterizes the interface between home and school for ethnic minority families. (Phenice, 1986. p.134

Juxtapositioning this contention with Ogbu's caste like analysis, sheds some light on why different teaching techniques are required for educating African-American children. In his analysis, Ogbu argues that because minority incorporation into the mainstream of American Society occurred involuntarily through forcible enslavement, conquest or incorporation of territory (as in the case of Native Americans)@, the economic and social rewards similar to those achieved by whites are not seen as a direct result of school or school achievements.

Why African- Americans Have a Different Frame of Reference About School

The literature on the history of education acknowledges that every child arrives in his or her first class at school with some preconceived notions that have historical and cultural relevance. That history includes social behavior and cognitive characteristics. For many African Americans, those characteristics include orientation towards people, ideas and things (Sade, 1982).

(Aschenbrenner,1973, Tolson and Wilson, (1990) see this type of orientation as establishing a caregiver relationship where the child seeks and expects to receive support within a network of relations. Furthermore, group oriented cultures such as that which permeate the African- American society value collectivity as opposed to competition (Boykin, 1986; Tolson and Wilson, 1990). Despite these well documented Aculturally based adaptive strengths (Nelson-LeGall, 1994:193), the transition to schooling has been difficult because most schools fail to incorporate these strengths into the learning process. In essence, cultural strengths do not translate into the development of effective tools for the African-American child. This is an educational crisis and the gravity of such crisis is not understood by many until questions are answered regarding the need to incorporate non Euroethnic techniques into learning. As a dogma in learning, Eurocentric constructs serves to strengthen and support European values and norms. The conceptual framework that is developed for learning using only European experiences minimizes and negates the strength of other culturally weighted learning methods.

Eurocentric Construct in Education

Gunnar Myrdal, (1944) summarizes Eurocentricity in the A American Creed , that is underlying what we seek to do is the belief in the rights and privileges regarded as ethically, morally and socially legitimate for all Americans. It appears therefore, that the American educational objective is derived from this American Dilemma. This approach make the rights, privileges and cultural imperatives of disadvantaged groups difficult to discern. Because of continuous cultivation of this dominant epistemological discourse, America has experienced such strives as the civil rights movement and the Black Muslim movement, all of which attempted with some significant success to introduce to America ideas that were different from those perceived in the American Creed. Pedagogical changes in the areas of communication or language are often ignored. White America still sees Blacks in ways different from themselves and structure language to reflect their perception in a subtle way. Fulton, (1972) points to the use of such verbiage as "black listed" or "black balled" or "Black Maria" or "Uncle Tom" or "Jewed down", all of which provoke emotions and reflect all that is bad in a condescending way. There are many aspects of the child's experience that are derived from the socialization process. (Bernstein, 1965) contends that when language is restrictive , A the imagination, curiosity and intellectual assertiveness of the African-American child is blunted and discouraged, as opposed to the elaborate form of communication which allows for a wider and more complex range of thought that is often associated with Eurocentric rationale. The language barrier facing the African-American child demotivates the child and discourages learning.

The poor African-American child has "seen less, read less, heard about less. His or her whole environment experience fewer changes than the socially privileged and he simply knows fewer possibilities." In support of this notion, (Adams and Friedrich, 1963) caution that unless the gap between the learning possibilities and the culture level of African Americans and whites are lessened, African- Americans will continue to lack the requisite motivation necessary to learn. When African-American children begin the formal learning process at school and fail to identify with any of the school's symbols, language of instructional delivery and examples used in teaching they will become less motivated because their background will not support or give meaning to such learning. They begin to expect less, and therefore often drop out of school.

Teaching is a noble profession which requires the constant pursuance of knowledge-consisting of new approaches to learning. Teachers have a responsibility to close the gap between what is practiced in the closed society and what is espoused in the open classroom (Fulton, 1972). When new, improved and inclusive teaching methods are proposed, there are echoes of resistance from educators who view the changes as an aberrant disregard for accepted and tested approaches. The question then becomes, tested for whom and on whom? If all children can learn, can they all learn in the same way? (Gardner, 1968) wrote in response to these questions that...the only road to development of a people is that of self development, including the right to make its own decision and its own mistakes , educate its own children in its own way, write its own poems and stories, revere its own Gods and heroes, choose its leaders and depose of them. If this is done, then each ethnic group in society with its own history, language and system of beliefs and behavior, and shapes the developmental process of the child.

Therefore, educational policies should be developed with the aim of enabling the social structure of the child and using that structure to enhance learning in a positive way. When strategies are developed that by passed this cultural imperative, it weakens the child and deprives the child of learning opportunities (Gaarder, 1968). Given this profound analysis by Gaarder, it appears that any debate about the relevance of the influence of the social environment on learning must take into consideration the differentiation in the background of the student. When teachers evaluate students = performance, they therefore, must do so with the understanding that this differentiation is not based on their own perception and expectations.

Extensive research has been conducted which links teacher expectation to student achievement and the evaluation of minority students is subject to A contamination ," especially when these students behave in a way that is a departure from commonly accepted norms. "Educators need to discover student's personal and ethnic strengths and avoid viewing cultural differences and deficits as disadvantages" (Brown, 1986). Because there is growing research on the perceived differential treatment of students from minority ethnic group and the continuous utilization of exclusive Euroethnic dominated teaching methods, values and beliefs. There is a need to suggest some possible changes. When asked for strategies for delimiting the effect of teaching and learning differentiation, many researchers readily offer the idea of multicultural or multiethnic education. While this concept has its strengths and weaknesses, recent intellectual work shows that its strengths are overwhelmingly significant. When feedback is provided as the theoretical and practical utility of multicultural education, the evidence seems to suggest that when complimented by pedagogical restructuring and curriculum adjustments, the results show the appearance of improved learning competencies in the acquisition of skills and knowledge and in the mastery of abilities. The selection of multiculturalism as an approach for incorporating non-European concepts into learning must not therefore, be seen as prejudicial but must be viewed within the contexts of the literature and its support for such an approach.

Multi cultural Education as a Learning Strategy

The debate over multicultural education rages on. Crowley and Garcia, (1994) prefer the concept of "education that is multicultural" to "multicultural education" because according to their analysis, the former calls for a total change in the structure of the education system and not just in the curriculum. But which ever way one views or defines "multiculturalism" one thing is clear, evidence in the literature show that multiculturalism dominates contemporary policy approaches for school reform. In 1989, for example, New York City followed other U. S. cities such as Portland, Omaha and Atlanta in responding to the call for multicultural education. The New York process consists of a detailed approach to providing students with education that is multi cultural. The New York experience delineates nine key areas for comprehensive change. They include curriculum development, program development, professional development, technical assistance, parental involvement, community involvement, affirmative action plan, program assessment/ evaluation and bilingual education. A Multicultural Advisory Board consisting of representatives from the religions, social and community organizations would design strategies for instructions, curriculum and professional development changes that meet individual district needs (New York City Board of Education, (19915). Several approaches for changes were suggested including the transformation- curriculum restructuring approach, additive-adding to the current curriculum and content and the social action approach which calls for societal changes to include the acceptance of differentiation in schooling (Banks, 1994). This comprehensive approach to change leads to what Banks calls a "multicultural school". According to Banks, this type of school would have eight characteristics, as shown in the table that follows.

VARIABLES	DESCRIPTION
Attitudes, perceptions, beliefs and actions of actions of school staff	The teachers and school administrators have expectations for all students and positive attitudes toward them in positive caring ways.
2. Formalized curriculum and course of study	The formalized curriculum reflects the experiences, culture and perspective of a range of cultural and ethnic groups as well as both genders.
3. Learning Teaching and Cultural Styles	The teaching styles used by the teachers match the learning, cultural and motivational styles of students.
4. Languages and Dialects of the School	The teachers and administrators show respect for the students= first language or dialect.
5. Instructional Materials	The instructional materials show events, situations and concepts from a wide range of ethnic, racial and cultural groups.
6. Assessment and Testing Procedures	The assessment and testing procedures used in the school are culturally sensitive and result in the student of color being represented

		proportionally in classes for gifted and talented.
7.	The School Culture and the Hidden Curriculum	The school culture and hidden curriculum reflect cultural and ethnic diversity.
8.	The Counseling Program	The school counselors have a high expectation of students from different racial, ethnic and language groups and help these students to set and realize positive career goals.

Adopted from: Banks, James A.(1994) <u>An Introduction to Multi cultural Education</u> Boston, Mass. : Allyn and Bacon, pp. 10-1

This conceptual framework summarizes the nature and content of a comprehensive framework for education that is multicultural. The framework also represents twenty years of work that has helped to shape the debate on the infusion of multicultural education into American schools (Banks, 1994: 7). Despite the convincing evidence in the literature, critics of multi cultural education still contend that it is a "glorified" framework for ethnic studies. But multi cultural education is not ethnic studies, it represents the broad view of the American Society and attempts to be inclusive of the diverse culture of which comprises America. (D, Souza, 1991 and Schlesinger, 1991) do not see ethnicity as a specific aspect of multiculturalism being institutionalized in American schools because conservative groups are fighting a fierce battle to keep it out. They do, however predict that "the days of Anglo hegemony in the U.S. Curriculum are limited."

OTHER STRATEGIES/ Early Intervention

Several studies have demonstrated the need for early intervention in learning as a means of introducing culturally sensitive values and norms into a child's learning repertoire. In 1977, the United States Office of Child Development presented evidence that early intervention works, that the impact of poverty on children can be overcome with appropriate treatment. In fact, several intervention programs have been used to demonstrate the importance and effectiveness of this strategy. Among them are the Washington, DC City of Lights Alternative School Program, the Boston Youth Build Program and the New York City Cullen Community Center Program.

In Washington, DC, the City of Lights Alternative School, founded in 1982 with support from the children's Defense Fund as part of a grant from the U.S. Department of Education provided comprehensive curriculum of instructions to children ages 12- 22, of which 98% are African-Americans and 70% are male. The curriculum is a tailored package and the curriculum includes education innovations, counseling, substance abuse prevention, job training and skills development among others. Because the program incorporated culturally sensitive issues and concepts into its curriculum, students with varied problems, expectations and aspirations excelled within that structure.

In Boston, Massachusetts, the Youth Build Boston Program, one of the fifteen affiliates of Youth Build USA, provides intensive one year work to school programs to many African-American students many of whom never completed high school, combining formal education with vocational strategies yielded tremendous success.

In New York City, where the Cullen Community Center operates a 24 hour and seven days a week program in Central Harlem district. Through this program, over three-hundred 5 to 19 year old participants are instructed in academic areas and provided cultural and spirited enrichment.

Dramatization and Play Making as a part of Learning

As pointed out by (Brickman and Lehrer,1972), many schools use "restrictive" rather than "elaborate" language in instructing African-American children. It is generally accepted in the literature that a child's environment provides early experiences upon which formal learning is based. This therefore, fuels the argument that because in the world of the poor African- American child, symbolism, creativity and group interaction dominate the home environment. If this is the case, it generally applies that any school environment that mimics that from where the child came is not only accommodating to the child, but enhances and reinforces learning. In other words "elaborate" language which calls for intensive deliberation borrows from the Euroethnic world view and is therefore, antithetical to the African-American world view. Dramatization, Play making and role playing all lead to discovery, they are also useful for skills training, problem solving and engender discussions of the logic of events, motives and characteristics. (Taba and Elkins, 1966: 84-85). Given this general explanation, those who may wish to argue with this strategy can see that there is no difference in the way which children learn. The learning process prescribed for the disadvantaged, minority or African-American child is subject to the same general principles of learning; that of proceeding from the concrete to the abstract. There is, however, a difference in "what is abstract and what is concrete to students who have gaps in their cognitive and verbal development and whose life experience may be limited in certain areas" as a result of their historical misfortune of which they had no control, this is where variations in teaching methods are necessary (Taba & Elkins, 1966).

CONCLUSION

In the current debate about improving the educational system for the diverse population of Americans, several issues are lost. Issues related to the continuous utilization of European centered examples, symbols and languages in explaining instructional phenomena are often considered factors that do not influence learning; factors that are disruptive and a departure from what the general society considers the best tools and diagnostic elements for producing a functionally literate individual. Attempts to introduce non-European concepts into learning are often seen by critics as radical and a call for educational equity of the civil rights era.

Some educators fret at the mere suggestion of reform because for them, cultural variation does not call for school reform, it only requires the child to adjust to a new learning environment. But what they fail to realize is that "cultural dissonance places students at risk of educational failure" Rossi, (1994:68). Noley, (1994) says it best when he points out that "European American efforts to assimilate native people throughout 500 years of European presence in North America have not been successful." Many native people including African Americans continue to value their culture and way of life but attempts by even well intentioned educators to reform American schools have ignored the "cultural validation issue." Certain structural adjustments have to be made in order to validate the culture of those who do not possess the Eurocentric background and, therefore do not benefit from its theoretical and empirical dominance in American educational discourse.

The implications of the continuous use of Eurocentric, Euroethnic or European concepts or constructs in delivering instructions in American schools is clear. The relationship in the paradigm that connects culture, behavior and general birth environment and experiences to school achievement should not be confused or misconceived. The debate is not over this relationship, and whether a relationship exist or does not exist is not a point of contention. What is continuously problematic is the reform needed to make schools more amenable to non-Eurocentric experiences as methods or strategies for teaching and learning. Beneath all of these semantics, the students who are to be the primary beneficiaries of the what the educational system has to offer continue to be cheated. They are cheated because their prior experiences have not fully been considered when designing educational programs. Until this case is resolved, it can be predicted that there will continue to exist what (Nelson-LeGall, 1994) calls the continuities and discontinuities between family and school for ethnic minority children

REFERENCES

Children's Defense Fund. (1990). AA Black Community Crusade and Covenant for Protecting Children@. Washington, DC: Children=s Defense Fund.

Adams, Fern and Friedrich, J. (Summer, 1963). ASummary of Literature and Development Guidelines for Diagnosis of Culturally Disadvantaged Pupils. Office of the Los Angeles County Superintendent of Schools, Division of Research and Guidance. p. 1.

Banks, James A. (1994). An Introduction to Multicultural Education. Boston, MA: Allyn and Bacon Publishers.

Bernstein, Basil. (January, 1965). AA Public Language: Some Sociological Implication of a Linguistic Form. British Journal of Sociology 10, pp.311- 327.

Boykin, A.W. (1986). "The Triple Quandary and the Schooling of Afro-American". In U. Neisser (Ed.). The School Achievement of Minority Children. Hillsdale, NJ: Erlbaum. pp.57-92

Brown, Thomas J. (1986). Teaching Minorities More Effectively A Model for Educators. Lanham, MD: University Press of America.

Brickman, William W. and Lehrer, Stanley. (1972). Education and the Many Faces of the Disadvantaged. New York: John Wiley and Sons, Inc.

Crowley, Pamela M. and Garcia, Maria L. (1994). "New Curriculum Developments: An Investigative Survey of New York City's Community School Districts Response to the Chancellor's Action Dean for Multicultural Education." In Rivera- Batiz, Francisco (Ed.). Reinventing Urban Education. New York: 1 Ume Press.

D'Souza, D. (1991). Liberal Education: The Politics of Race and Sex on Campus. New York: Free Press.

Gaarder, Bruce A. (1968). AEducation of America Indian Children, In James E. Alatis (Ed.). Monograph Series on Languages and Linguistics. pp. 83-86.

Lazarfeld, Paul as quoted in Genevieve Knupfer, "Portrait of the Underdog." in Class Status and Power (Ed.) (1963) by Reinhard Bendix and Seymour Lipset Glencoe, Illinois: Free Press, pp. 263.

Myrdal, Gunner. (1944). An American Dilemma. New York: Harper, pp.xlv- xlvii

Nelson-LeGall , Sharon. (1994). "Addressing the Continuities and Discontinuities Between Family and School for Ethnic Minority Children" in Rivera- Batiz, Francisco (Ed.). Reinventing Urban Education. New York: 1 UME Press.

New York City Board of Education. (1991). An Action Plan for Multicultural Education. New York:

Noley, Grayson. (1994). "The Cultural Context of American Indian Education and Arts Relevance to Educational Reform Efforts". In Rossi, Robert. Schools and Students at Risk: Context and Framework for Positive Change. New York: Teachers College Press.

Ogbu, J. (1978). Minority Education and Caste: The American System in Cross-Cultural-Perspective. Minority Education and Caste: The American System in Cross-Cultural Perspective. New York: Academic Press.

Olsen, Edward G. (1972) "Teacher Competencies for Work with Culturally Different Children and Youth." In Brickman, William and Lehrer, Stanley (Ed.). Education and the Many Faces of the Disadvantaged. New York: John Wiley and Sons, Inc.

Phenice, I. and et al.(1986). A Minority Family Agendas: The Home-School Interface and Alternative Schooling Models. In R. Griffore and R. Boger (Eds.). Child Rearing in the Home and School. New York: Plenum, pp. 121-156.

Rossi, Robert J.(1994). Schools and Students at Risk: Context and Framework for Positive Change. New York: Teachers College Press.

Sade, B.(1982) "Afro-American Cognitive Style: A Variable in School Success?" Review ofEducational Research.52, pp.219-244

Schlesinger, A. (1991). The Disuniting of America: Reflections on a Multicultural Society. Knoxville: Whittle Direct Books.

Taba, Hilda and Elkins, Deborah. (1966). Teaching Strategies for the Culturally Disadvantaged. Chicago: Rand McNally and Co.

Tolson, T. and Wilson, M. (1990)."The Impact of Two and Three Generational Black Family Structure on Perceived Family Climate". <u>Child Development</u>, 61, pp. 416-428.

Chapter Five

Respectful Education for All Children

Barbara Trzcinski
Livonia, MI

The place of poverty can have a profound affect on learning. This affect is not because of disinterest but because of the concomitant conditions of poverty. Poor nutrition and hunger can cause low levels of concentration. Anxiety and worry about living conditions and family interfere with classroom focus. Overcrowded conditions make relaxation and sound sleep difficult and provide a poor foundation for school. Coming to school requires a lot of motivation if you are tired or hungry or worried. It is important to honor that motivation with respect for the child and provide helpful opportunities for learning to uplift that child and their family.

In the Classroom:

Children of poverty may not be following through on assignments or participating in class because they may lack the resources. Perhaps the reason a child has not completed the posterboard illustration to accompany the story read in class is because they do not have access to obtaining a posterboard or related materials because of no transportation or no money. Such a project would also require working space that be unavailable for a child living in crowded or transient conditions. The teacher may consider providing a work space within the classroom for all children to use that has the material necessary. Alternatively, allow children time to make an appointment with the art teacher to use those materials to complete the project.

Assignments that require adult assistance or supervision in the evening are unfair for children who may not have an adult available. Many children have parents who are working in the evenings and need to take their children with them because of lack of childcare. Other children may have adults who have worked hard all day at low-paying jobs and are too exhausted to attend to anything that is not essential to daily living. The adult at the end of the day that is too difficult is frustrated and may produce the opposite result of the hoped for opportunity of family time. The teacher may consider providing a range of methods to complete an assignment to accommodate for lack of adult help.

Trips to the library may be impossible for some children. The teach may have the resources available in school that are needed for the research project. Consider providing free transportation for students and their families, perhaps as a library field trip on Saturdays with a return visit when the books are due. The library may have a mobile unit that could bring a specific books related to the subjects studied encouraging reading by all family members builds a school community.

Math assignments can be creative ways to help families. Cooking requires measuring, which is math. Mixes that require only water, such a Jell-O or muffin mixes provide a useful assignment if students have a stove available at home. Students with more transient conditions, such as homeless children in shelters, or students who lack an available adult, may need ready made items that can be cut into servings, using estimating and fraction skills. Cooking in school as part of math could allow a student to take home a family treat.

Our senior citizens are one of this country's greatest untapped resources. Connect with a local senior citizens group to establish a volunteer program. Individual reading with an adult can assist a child with early literacy difficulties. Math games can be played during recess with an adult volunteer. Relationships between senior citizens and children benefit everyone.

Honor students at high schools need community service points as part of their Honor Society membership. Individual tutoring or a study club supervised after school can support students. Having the tutoring or study club held at the school rather than in individual homes typically increases the safety and convenience of volunteers.

The teacher could provide enrichment material or references for students to take home. Kindergarten "round-up" in the Spring is an easy time to give books, magnetic letters or math games that can help a child prepare for the next school year. Households with limited income often cannot allocate funds for books or reference material.

Read stories about individuals who have achieved despite great odds. The only difference between a goal and a dream is a plan. Help students write their own stories about what they want to achieve and then assist in making a plan for reaching that goal.

Developing mentor relationships with professionals in the community that can show students what various jobs encompass. Students with particular gifts could be paired with a professional in an occupation that requires those talents.

In the Larger School Environment

Develop a parent liaison position for someone to focus on getting to know families and acting as a friendly representative of the school. This position does not include any discipline or administrative authority but should act as a bridge of understanding. When children have difficulty in school, the parent liaison may be able to assist the school in understanding the reason for the difficulty and offer suggestions regarding school support to meet the family's needs.

Health issues affect the learning and are often sources of stress for families. Health insurance is often out of reach for families. Work with the public health department to establish a school based immunization clinic. Develop a free health clinic within the school for families. There may be specific funding for addressing health issues.

A school "store" where children can "buy" items with points earned by good behavior can obtain practical items. Lightweight, non perishable food items than a cute gadget that is useless. Of course, children should receive a sticker or fun pencil as a bonus for shopping.

A quiet, empty school building is a sad sight. Areas of poverty are frequently ignored in terms of resources for entertainment. A school can be positive place for entertainment as well learning. Encouraging families to have fun together in a cost-free environment is good for family and community development as well as portrays the school as a friendly and accepting place. Local merchants or churches will often donate items to schools. Grants can be written to fund activities. The mayor's office may also be a resource. A variety of programs can be easily provided:

- Family fun nights can focus on math or science. Many hands-on museums have mobile units that can set up activities that incorporate fun and learning.

- Multicultural nights can be based on each classroom's social studies project focusing on a particular country. Displays and food samples in the hallway provide a festive atmosphere that leads to awareness of others and learning. Teachers and families are great resources for cultural artifacts.

- Parenting fairs can provide free samples of health and safety items given out at the end of the night in appreciation for attending. School personnel, such as the school psychologist or social worker can provide sessions on growth and development issues or parenting skills. The teacher of speech and language impaired students can discuss normal speech development and ways to stimulate good speech patterns. The school nurse can speak to medical issues and low cost ways to ensure good family nutrition. Large legal firms often have a pro bono budget that can be tapped.

- Pasta nights or ice cream socials allow families to eat and share together. Held after a playground or neighborhood clean up effort, families come proudly rather than for a hand-out.

- Honor award assemblies that children can invite their families to attend allows a celebration. Honoring students for good behavior, motivation, effort or helpfulness provides a sense of pride and achievement.

Conclusion

Ideas that can be useful in reaching children of poverty are useful for all children. All families benefit from a positive and accepting school environment that is interested in supporting their needs and working with them as a team to help them achieve their goals. When accommodation are made within the environment as a whole, and offered to all, no particular child or family is singled out. Respectful education requires treating children and families equally by adequately meeting their individual needs.

CHAPTER 6

ASSISTING POVERTY-STRICKEN STUDENTS THROUGH EARLY IDENTIFICATION, SOUND INSTRUCTIONAL PRACTICES, AND MODIFIED CONTENT AREA READING STRATEGIES

Glynn Travis King
Assistant Professor
Albany State University
Albany, GA

THE GENERAL STATE OF POVERTY STRICKEN STUDENTS

Scenario

You've graduated from college with a teaching degree in secondary English, you've had your interview with the school superintendent, you've been given a tour of the school by the principal, and finally, you've been offered a job as a remedial reading teacher in a poverty-stricken, rural community. Great! Wait a minute, you've been trained to be an English teacher, and you've only had one reading course. The scenario I have just described happened to me. Furthermore, I have the feeling that I'm not the only English teacher ever offered that kind of teaching position. By the way, I accepted the position, and I taught there for two years before leaving to pursue my master's degree in reading education.

This chapter is a combination of the practical experiences I have gained from years of teaching poverty stricken students in remedial reading classes in every grade from fifth to twelfth and the additional insights gleaned from years of academic study which led to my doctorate in reading education. Throughout the chapter, when reading terms are used, a bold print contextual definition will be offered in that sentence.

The Prime Causal Factor in the Academic Failure
of Poverty Stricken Students

As a remedial reading teacher in middle and secondary schools, the one question I found most difficult to answer was, "How do students get so far behind in their reading skills?" The difficulty in answering this question came from the fact that, as with most things in life, there are many factors that affect a student's academic progress. To be honest, I wasn't sure which factor had the greatest impact on my poverty-stricken eighth and ninth graders who read at a third or fourth grade level. I knew that being poor meant having to deal with problems such as substandard housing, neighborhood violence, despair, and unemployment

(Mickelson & Smith,1989) plus a host of other problems. However, after years of pondering this question, I believe the main reason most poverty-stricken students fall behind their classmates is their lack of verbal interactions with adults.

The lack of verbal interactions in the first four or five years of life causes most poverty stricken students to start far behind their classmates in academics. This subtle form of neglect by parents or guardians is evident in the children's lack of expressive and receptive language. More than likely this does *not* mean these children are lacking in intellectual ability. Instead, I believe this lack of language ability indicates that these students have not had a stable adult in their lives who talked to and listened to them. In essence, they have missed out on the first four or five critical years of language training in a home setting. Because of this neglect, many poverty stricken students enter pre-kindergarten or kindergarten not knowing the alphabet, the colors, their address, or even their real name. Some are so stunted in their language acquisition that their attempts at expressing themselves are unintelligible. *More importantly, without adequate language skills, these students do not master the reading skills necessary for success in school and life. The foundation of their failure is laid in the first four years of neglect.* If this is the prime causal factor for their academic failure, then more efforts should be made to identify and rescue students with these negative home environments. It seems plausible that this type of intervention would be more effective than the current push to eliminate the problem by "fixing" the teacher.

What Happens to Poverty Stricken Students at School

Most of these poverty-stricken students never "catch up" with their classmates who had the benefits of language training in their early years. In the school setting, these victims of poverty face years of failure and humiliation. They become experts at avoiding teachers when it is time to call on someone to read. Many are socially promoted without the skills necessary for success. Others drop out or cut up and get kicked out rather than face the daily fear of being called on to read. Even social promotion is a false hope because it ends with their freshman year (ninth grade) in high school. In the ninth grade, for the first time in their schooling experience, these socially promoted students are required to pass a required number of Carnegie units for promotion. In twenty-three states, the small percentage of poverty stricken students who have the minimal language abilities to make it through all twelve years of public schooling are now being faced with an "exit exam" (U.S. Department of Education, 1994). Some never make it past this last barrier to a high school diploma.

What is Being Done to Assist Poverty Stricken Students

In general, far too little is being done to assist poverty stricken students achieve success in the school setting. Many states are choosing to attack the *results* of poverty rather than its *causes*. The leaders in these states believe the answer lies in setting higher standards to motivate higher achievement. They have taken the statement by former Secretary of Education, Terrence Bell, in A Nation at Risk (1984) that we have "dumbed down the text" as a justification for setting the academic bar at one level and expecting every student to jump over it. This "holier than thou" "I had a good home, why didn't you" attitude does not recognize individual differences or the value of differentiated instruction. While "raising the bar" may have a positive effect on students from financially stable homes, it will probably have a negative effect on students who have been crippled by the poverty of their home environment.

Positive News for Poverty Stricken Students

I applaud the state of Georgia for two outstanding programs that will aid poverty stricken students, the Pre-kindergarten Program and the Hope Scholarship Program. Both programs are funded through lottery funds that are designated by law for these programs.

The first program, the Pre-kindergarten program, is free to four-year olds. That means no childcare fees for parents to pay that year. This program teaches language and problem solving skills plus a host of other cognitive skills. I have marveled at my son's Pre-K teacher and paraprofessional as they interact with the class and lead them through the lessons for the day. I have noted how the teacher and the paraprofessional have assisted less-able students in understanding directions and in expressing themselves verbally. Since several of these students come from poverty-stricken, dysfunctional homes where they receive little or no attention, the pre-kindergarten program provides the intellectual stimulation lacking in these dysfunctional homes. One sad incident gave me a better understanding of the negative effects of dysfunctional homes. While assisting the young boys in my son's Pre-K class in washing their hands, one young boy came to me, tugged on my sleeve, and said, "I can't go home." When I asked him why, he said, "Mommy said we go hotel because Daddy angry with her (sic)." I explained the situation to the teacher and suggested the young man see a counselor. My heart broke as I contemplated the emotional toll this home situation will have on this sweet, innocent four year old boy.

The second program, the Hope Scholarship program (1-800-546-HOPE), provides forgivable loans for high achieving students who aspire to teach in Georgia. These students must have a minimum overall grade point average of 3.6 on a 4.0 scale. The maximum award for a full-time student is $3,000 for the junior year and another $3,000 for the senior year. This $6,000 stipend will be a great boon to all academically able students, but it will impact those students from poverty stricken homes the most. This program will open the door that had previously been closed by dire economic circumstances. Frankly, with the financial incentives offered by this program, I am surprised some people have not moved to Georgia to reap these benefits.

EARLY IDENTIFICATION OF POVERTY STRICKEN STUDENTS

How Teachers Can Identify Their Poverty Stricken Students

At the beginning of the school year, I have my middle grades and secondary students do some type of seatwork like filling out forms. Next, I ask all my students to take out their textbook and turn to a certain page. I walk around with my seating chart in my hand and quietly ask each student to read a little out loud for me. With three or four students, it is painfully obvious that they do not have a sight vocabulary and they cannot read the textbook. I circle these students' names on my seating chart. They become my challenge for that year. I know that if I do not help them probably no one else will. With early childhood students, I suggest that teachers walk around with a list of the alphabet (upper and lower case) which has been written out of order or a Dolch Sight Word List (Dolch, 1942). I believe as teachers ask their students to identify the alphabet and words on the sight word list, they will be able to recognize the neglected and poverty stricken students. Finally, I recommend teachers go to the guidance counselor's office and read the file on their students who are struggling in class. It is a well kept secret that teachers are allowed access to their students' files. In fact, one of the main purposes for keeping files is to assist teachers in understanding their students.

How Teachers Can Assist Their Poverty Stricken Students

When teachers realize they have students in their classroom who are far behind the other students, they have two choices. They can continue covering the material to be taught without any adaptations and watch the students fail or they can think of alternative ways to get the material across while teaching the missing skills and watch the hope return to their students' eyes. The first few years I taught, I did the former because I did not know how to assist these students who were so far behind.

There are several ways that teachers can aid their poverty-stricken students in their interactions with textbooks. I will only mention a few. One easy way to ensure that every student can read their text is to provide them with **an audiotape of the textbook** that they can listen to while reading the text. Most people's listening capacity is higher than their reading capacity. A good example of this is the first time I encountered the word "hors d'oeuvre" in print. I didn't realize it meant the little appetizers served at parties. Many poverty stricken students react the same way only with more commonly understood words. Since teachers are overburdened already with a myriad of tasks they are expected to perform, I suggest they offer extra credit to their able readers who have averages in the high 90s and who will do anything for a 100 average. Simply give these students a tape recorder with a blank tape in it and ask them to tape themselves reading a chapter with all its headings and subheadings. When the students bring the tapes back, I suggest the teacher take the tape and several blank tapes to the local library and ask them to make copies. Then, when the class is reading, the teacher can have less able readers put on headphones and listen to the tape as they read. The tape assists the less able readers in learning the material and will bolster their sight vocabulary.

Additional means of assisting poverty stricken students in interacting with the textbook are: **paired reading partners** (Larson & Danserear, 1986), **peer tutors, a contextual dictionary created specifically for the classroom text and familiarizing students with text at the first of the year**. First, with **paired reading partners**, I wait until I know which pairs of students will likely get along in a paired reading setting before I set up a separate seating chart for paired readings. Research by Devin-Sheehan, Feldman, & Allen (1976) recommends pairing students of same sex and similar abilities. With middle grades and secondary students, same sex pairings make sense to me because if you pair a male student with a female student you bring in a host of other distracting factors. For instance, one student may not want the other student to know how much difficulty he or she has reading. Pairing students who are close in ability makes sense because I have paired a high ability student with a less able student only to realize that they did not talk the same language and the high ability student became frustrated with the less able student's slowness in learning.

Second, **peer tutors** can be successful with poverty-stricken students if teachers are willing to view cooperative learning as a positive learning tool. For years, I, like many other teachers, worried that using peer tutors was like helping the less able student cheat. Then, I realized that I was helping them overcome the years of neglect and the lack of home support. In essence, I was leveling the playing field.

Third, an entire class can take on the project of creating **a contextual dictionary for the class text**. As the class reads through the text, the students identify the difficult words on each page and write a short definition that matches the context of the passage. The teacher can then make several copies available so less able students can look up the word and find the exact definition for how the word is used on that page.

Finally, in the rush to start teaching, many teachers fail to take class time to **familiarize their students with the organization of the text**. Some form of preliminary surveying of the text should be undertaken so the students get the big picture before more intensive study takes place. I recommend creating an exercise to prompt students to find pertinent information in their text. I make this recommendation based on the fact that I have had many students in my reading classes who did not know how to use the index and who were not aware of the glossary in their content area textbooks.

SOUND INSTRUCTIONAL PRACTICES

I would like to recommend five sound instructional practices that facilitate learning and long-term retention. I recommend these practices because I am convinced that many teachers are more concerned with covering the material than they are with ensuring learning takes place. When teachers tell me they need to cover the text I am tempted to give them a brown paper bag and some tape. Research by Ebbinghaus (1908) verifies that, in only a few days, students forget up to 60 or 70 percent of the information they have learned in class. On the other hand, Peters and Levin (1986) found that using a simple thing like mnemonics benefited the memory of both above-and-below-average readers. I believe the omission of the following five sound instructional practices accounts for a great portion of forgotten information.

The first sound instructional practice is to check for immediate recall as soon as you teach something. After each teaching session, teachers should have students turn their notes over so the teacher can check right then how much of the material was retained. If very little information was retained, re-teaching should take place.

The second, and possibly most important sound instructional practice, is what I call "spaced review." This means frequently reviewing the material that has previously been taught. The opposite approach is to go straight through the text with little or no reviews or to teach every vocabulary lesson in the text without ever looking back at the previous lessons. Because so many teachers neglect this practice, I teach my pre-service teachers that the three best ways to teach are repetition, repetition, and (Let's see, there's one more. Oh yes! Repetition!) Then I remind them to ask good questions to prompt critical thinking. To get my point across, I ask my students how many can sing a song all the way through the first time they hear it. When no hands are raised, I then comment that I can't do that either. Then I tell my class if I hear the song about thirty times I find myself singing it in the shower. A lot of repetition is needed for initial learning and, more specially, to move something from short term to long term memory. Most poverty-stricken students do not have someone at home who reviews their work at school to move it into long-term memory. That is why I believe in the next sound instructional practice.

The third sound instructional practice is beginning each class with a review of the lessons of the previous day. These daily reviews bring continuity to the lessons and aid in retention of material covered. So, I advise teachers who are not sure how to start the lesson for the day to remember they can always review what they taught yesterday.

The fourth sound instructional practice is to teach or review content area terms/vocabulary every day. I am afraid that many math, science, language arts, and social science teachers assume that their students know the terms particular to the subject area. This erroneous belief is called "assumptive teaching." The military taught me to break down "assume" into the following three parts

"ASS/U/ME" so I would remember that when people assume without knowing they make an "donkey" out of you and me.

The fifth sound instructional practice is to work assignments with students rather than assigning them to students. I advise my pre-service students to do the first couple of items on every exercise to model how the exercise should be done. In addition, I encourage doing the first item on every test so no one gets it wrong. I always hated starting a test with the realization that I didn't even know the first item. Doing the first couple of items on exercises so students can see how they are done is in keeping with Bandura's (1965) modeling theory.

How to Make Oral Reading a Non-Threatening Activity

In my teaching career, I have tried to implement the following principles which I believe make oral reading less threatening to my poverty stricken, less able readers. **The first principle for making oral reading easy is to establish the fact that no one (student or teacher) will laugh at or correct anyone who reads out loud in class.** Some students will be cruel to other students if the teacher does not make it clear that dire consequences will fall upon any student who does not follow this rule. If a student laughs at a reader and the teacher fails to figuratively "nail that student to the cross," then other students will fear ridicule when they read. Soon, only the very confident readers will want to read out loud in class. Fear of embarrassment will rule the class. To encourage my students to refrain from criticizing each other, I explain that there are two types of people in this world, those who lift you up and those who pull you down. I go on to explain that those that lift you up are called "friends" and those who pull you down are called a couple of words I can't say in public.

The second principle for making oral reading easy is to place students in materials that are on or below their reading level. I have found that the most frustrated, less able readers will read if I find materials that are easy for them to read. In fact, during the first week of school, many of my students are hesitant to read out loud in class. After the first week of reading classes, when my students realize they can read the materials I have, they start asking to read. Now, for content area teachers **(math, science, language arts, and social studies)**, it is more difficult to find materials written at two levels. Here are some things I have tried with content area classes. I have raided the book room in an effort to find easier texts that cover the same material. I have searched for publishers who offer different levels of the same text, and I have called publishers to find high/low materials **(high interest/low readability)**. If these efforts fail, I would ask some of my more able readers to tape record chapters of the text so the less able readers can read the chapter while it is being read to them.

The third principle for making oral reading easy is to read alternating sentences with your students until you determine who can read larger sections of text with ease. At the beginning of the year, I tell my students that in my class they will only have to read one sentence and I will read the next sentence. In other words, I will read a sentence; they will read a sentence; I will read a sentence; they will read a sentence, and I will call on someone else. I read with my class in this manner until I identify my less able readers. Less able readers get really nervous when asked to read a lot of connected text. So, if you choose to call on students who happens to be less able readers and ask them to read a paragraph or a page, they will be embarrassed in front of the whole class and your car will probably be "keyed" at the end of the day. Additionally, I tell my class that if they encounter a word they don't know while reading orally, they should stop and I will pronounce it for them. I joke with them by saying they pay me extra for every student I help. When a student encounters a difficult word, I choose to pronounce it for them rather than clap out the syllables or stop them in the middle of the sentence to teach word identification skills (context, configuration, dictionary skills, phonics, picture skills, sight words, structural analysis, and syllabication).

The forth principle for making oral reading easy is to let students know that you are going to ask them questions over what they read orally before they start reading. Let me give you an example that might clarify this principle. I have been called on to read orally while attending a Sunday school class. After I have read and correctly pronounced every biblical name, the teacher has said, "Now, Travis, tell us what that means to you?" Immediately, I try to silently skim over the material I have just read orally in an attempt to understand what I have read. Many students do exactly what I have done in the example above. When they are called on to read orally, they are so intent on not mispronouncing any words that they neglect to attend to meaning. However, when I say, "George, read the next paragraph for us, but think about it because I'm going to ask you some questions over it," George realizes he must attend to pronunciation and meaning and he does not give me that stricken look that I gave the Sunday school teacher.

MODIFIED CONTENT AREA READING STRATEGIES

Four long-accepted content area reading strategies that I have found to be tried-and-true, List-Group-Label (Taba, 1967), the ReQuest Procedure (Manzo, 1969), the Guided Reading Procedure (Manzo, 1975), and Radio Reading (Greene, 1979), need some modifications to be effective with poverty-stricken, less-able readers. The first strategy, **List - Group - Label**, is Taba's classification technique that allows students to organize information they have read and then compare their organization with their classmates' organizations. It has four steps. In step one, the students read part of a text and then select a broad topic from their reading selection. In step two, the teacher writes the topic on the board and solicits terms from the class that would fit under the topic selected. In step three, the students organize the terms they have generated into groups that have something in common and give these groups a label. In step four, the students explain their groupings and explain the rationale behind their choices.

In my modification of List-Group-Label, I use the strategy as a pretest and posttest. Before my class studies a chapter, I select a topic that we are going to study about, and I write that topic on the board. I tell my students that we are going to play a game with the topic that will tell me how much they know about the topic. If I have a joking relationship with the class, I may say it shouldn't take long with this class. I go on and explain that the game has two simple rules. Rule one is "If you know anything about the topic, raise your hand and tell us. Rule two is "If one of your classmates says something that is related to the topic and you don't understand how it is related, raise your hand and your classmate or I will explain the relationship. If everyone understands the rules, I get the class to list everything they can think of related to the topic. I always use a scribe (a student whom I trust to write on the board for me) to write everything the students say, even things which may not be related to the topic. This is the List part of the technique. Next I ask my students to look at the terms we have generated to identify a group of terms that are all related to the topic in the same way. This is the Group part of the technique. Finally, I ask my students to create a label that explains how these terms are related. As a brief example, suppose we are about to study the Civil War. After the list is made, the student may form groups such as battles, weapons, nicknames, southern generals, and northern generals. I keep this pretest list and compare it with the posttest list in an effort to determine the depth of learning that has taken place.

The second strategy, **the ReQuest Procedure,** is Manzo's method of helping students develop a questioning skill approach to textbook reading. ReQuest, which stands for "reciprocal questioning" is a seven-step procedure. In the first step, the students and teacher silently read a common segment of the text. In the second step, the teacher closes the text and is questioned about the segment by the students. In the third step, the teacher queries the students about the segment read. In the fourth step, another segment of the text is read, and steps two and three are repeated. In the fifth step, the teacher starts asking prediction questions. In the sixth step, the teacher assigns to remainder of the selection to be read silently. In the seventh step, the teacher discusses the selection.

In my modification of the ReQuest Procedure, I use the strategy as a means of modeling higher-level questions in dealing with a text while challenging my class to a comprehension duel. I challenge my class by saying, "I have a challenge for you. Let's read the next two pages of the text silently. When you finish, please turn your text face down, and I will do the same. When I get through reading, you can ask me any question you have on these two pages. In fact, while you are reading, write down any question you want to ask me with the page and paragraph where the answer is found. The only catch is when you get through asking me questions, I'm going to ask you questions." Some students who are not motivated by the text will be motivated to "stump" the teacher. For this procedure to be effective, the teacher must read the text looking for higher level questions and places to stop and make predictions.

In the **ReQuest** Procedure, my students will ask only one or two to the four types of questions. I try to model all four types of questions. I was taught that the four basic types of questions are recall, convergent, divergent, and value. An example of a "recall" question is, "How many home runs did Hank Aaron hit? The answer is found in the text. With convergent, divergent, and value questions, the answer is not stated in the text. An example of a "convergent" question is, "If Jim threw down his bat, kicked the water cooler, and leaned against the dugout with his bottom lip stuck out, in what mood would he be? There is one correct answer to a convergent question. Two examples of a "divergent" question are, "What would the United States be like if the South had won the Civil War?" and "What do you think transportation will be like in fifty years?" There is not one correct answer to a divergent question. An example of a "value" question is, "Do you agree or disagree with the decision to inter Japanese-Americans during World War II?

The third strategy, **the Guided Reading Procedure**, is Manzo's way of conducting a whole-class brainstorming activity after reading a section of a text. It has eight steps. In the first step, the teacher prepares the students for reading by clarifying key concepts. In the second step, the teacher assigns a 500-900 word selection for middle school students or a 1,000-2,000 word selection for high school students with the directions, "Read to remember all you can." In the third step, the students turn their book face down as they finish reading the material. The teacher asks them what they remember and records their remembrances on the board. In the fourth step, helps the students recognize that there is much they have not remembered or have remembered incorrectly. In the fifth step, the teacher sends the students back to the text to correct erroneous information and to add new information. In the sixth step, the teacher helps the students organize the information on the board. In the seventh step, the teacher asks questions that will stimulate an analysis of the material and a synthesis of the ideas with previous learning. In the eighth step, the teacher provides immediate feedback in the form of a short quiz.

In my modification of the Guided Reading Procedure, I say to my students, "Let's read the next two pages silently and then see how much we can remember." As we record our remembrances, I use a scribe because I like keeping eye contact with my class. I try to call on my less able students first so they can contribute without having the more able students "steal their thunder." My main modification is I use lots of praise as the students remember ideas from the text.

The fourth strategy, **Radio Reading**, is Greene's method of teaching listening skills through oral reading. It has five steps. In the first step, the teacher assigns the text material and does pre-reading preparation. In the second step, the teacher forms small groups. In the third step, as each reader reads, the other students have their books closed. In the fourth step, the teacher initiates discussion by asking each member of the group a question about the material read. In the fifth step, each student takes a turn as a reader.

My only modification of Radio Reading is that I use the procedure with the whole class. I like the fact that when a student makes a mistake reading orally, the other students are not able to jump on the mistake. In addition, I like the procedure because it is one of the few listening exercises I use regularly.

SUMMARY

One of the most controversial problems in schools is how to reach students who come from families living at or below the poverty line (Alvermann & Phelps, 1994). The problem is not a small one. According to the National Center for Educational Statistics (1992), 44 percent of African-American children and 38 percent of Hispanic children fit into this category. If we, as teachers, are to help these students reach their full potential, we must adapt our instruction to meet their special needs. Unfortunately, many of these students are socially promoted without the adaptations they need so each year the gap widens between what they can read and what they are asked to read. Eventually the gap becomes so large that school becomes a place of failure that prompts anger and frustration. Unless we, as teachers, reach these students through early identification, assistance in dealing with textbooks, sound educational practices, and modified content area reading strategies, they will become "unproductive, underdeveloped, and noncompetitive" Pellicano (1987). If this happens, they may become so hopeless that they become a danger to themselves and to us.

References

Alvermann, D. E., & Phelps, S. F. (1994). *Content reading and Literacy: Succeeding in today's diverse classrooms.* Needham Heights, MA: Allyn and Bacon.

Bandura, A. (1965). *Behavior modification through modeling procedures.* In L. Krasner & L. P. Ullmann (Eds.) Research in behavior modification (pp. 310-340) New York: Holt, Rinehart and Winston.

Bell, T. (1983). *A Nation at Risk.* Washington, DC: U. S. Government Printing Office.

Devin-Sheehan, L., Feldman, R. S., & Allen, V. L. (1976). *Research on children tutoring children: A critical review.* Review of Educational Research, 46(3), 355-385.

Dolch, E. W. (1973). *Basic sight word test.* Champaign, IL: Garrard Press

Ebbinghaus, H. (1908). *Abriss der Psychologie* (M. Meyer, Trans. and Ed.). New York: Arno Press, 1973.

Greene, F. P. (1970). *Paired reading.* Unpublished paper, Syracuse University. Discusses the rationale and implementation of another version of Paired Reading.

Larson, C., & Danserear, D. (1986). Cooperative learning in dyads. Journal of Reading, 29, 516-520.

Manzo, A. V. (1969). *The ReQuest procedure.* Journal of Reading, 11, 123-126.

Manzo, A. V. (1975). *The guided reading procedure.* Journal of Reading, 18, 287-291.

Mickelson, R. A., & Smith, S. S. (1989). Inner-city dislocations and school outcomes: A structural interpretation. In G. L. Berry & J. K. Asamen (Eds.), Black Students: Psychological issues and academic achievement (pp. 99-119). Newbury Park, CA: Sage Publications.

National Center for Education Statistics. (1992b, June). *The condition of education.* Washington, DC: U. S. Government Printing Office.

Peters, E. E., & Levin, J. R. (1986). *Effect of a mnemonic imagery strategy on good and poor readers' prose recall.* Reading Research Quarterly, 21, 179-192.

Pellicano, R. (1987). *At-risk: A view of "social advantage."* Educational Leadership, 44, 47-50.

Taba, H. (1967). Teacher's Handbook for Elementray Social Studies. Reading, MA: Addison-Wesley.

U. S. Department of Education. (1998). *Key State Education Policies on K-12 Education.* Washington, DC: U. S. Government Printing Office.

CHAPTER 7

ATTITUDES AND EXPERIENCES OF COLLEGE STUDENTS ON DOMESTIC VIOLENCE

Nearly half of homeless children either have been evolved or have been subjected to violence in their home.

Renee Wallace, Ph.D.
Associate Professor
Albany State University
Albany, Georgia

Recent public perception of "widespread" domestic violence has captured the attention of many Americans. There is a growing demand for more research and violence prevention programs to reduce aggression and victimization. A report from the National Crime Survey by the U. S. Bureau of the Census reported that approximately 3,000,000 incidents of crime and violence are reported annually for grades K-12 (Stephens, 1991). An estimation of approximately 1 million teenagers between 12 and 19 are raped, robbed, or assaulted annually (Kantrowitz, 1993). In 1992, a report from the National Association of School Security Directors state that approximately 9,000 rapes, 12, 000 armed robberies, 270,000 burglaries, and 204,000 aggravated assaults occurred in the United States schools (Rich, 1992).

In 1993, the Federal Bureau of Investigation reported that a crime is committed every two seconds in the United States; moreover, a property crime is committed every three seconds and a violent crime every twenty-one seconds. However, in spousal or domestic abuse cases, the National Crime Victimization Survey of the U. S. Department of Justice indicated that between 1987-1991, 61,000 rapes, robberies or assaults occurred. Of this figure, 90 percent were committed against females by spouses, ex-spouses, or boyfriends (Zawitz, 1994).

According to a recent study by Moon, ET, at. (1996), a woman is battered every 18 seconds and more than half of all women will experience some form of violence from their spouse during marriage. In addition, over 3.3 million children witness domestic violence each year and of those children who witness violence in the home, 50 percent of the girls will become victims and 60 percent of the boys will become batterers. Eighty percent of all people in prison grew up in violent homes and sons who witness abuse are ten times likely to abuse their partners.

Jaffee (1986) found in a study of 46 witnesses of domestic violence that 20 percent were truant, 16 percent had been in court, 50 percent acted out in school, 30 percent acted out with peers/teachers, and 57 percent were below average or had failing grades in school. In a study of acquaintance rape, Burkhart (1983) indicated that almost two-thirds of college males admitted to fondling females against their will, and one-half admitted to force sexual activity. Also, Butler (1996) stated that 50 percent of all teenagers believe it is okay to force sex.

Social learning theory studies indicate that children are influenced by aggressive models and data from peer group influence studies show that children learn by watching and emulating others, especially those who are of the same sex and who are close to them (Bandura, 1973).

Many behaviors of children and adolescents are also associated with the "so-called" role models in the athletic arena. In particularly, contact and collision sports (e.g., football, hockey, basketball, and wrestling) are associated with violence and sometimes the rhetoric is generalized to women. For example, the following comments were made by highly respected and influential sports figures:

- Joe Patero, football coach at Penn State University after losing to the University of Texas in September, 1990, "Well, I'm going to have to go home and beat my wife."

- Charles Barkley, professional basketball player (formerly for the Philadelphia 76ers in 1990) after a loss to the New Jersey Nets, Said, "you just go home and beat your wife and kids after this."

- Bobby Knight, basketball coach at the University of Indiana, "I think that if rape is inevitable, relax and enjoy it."

Although there are few studies that document domestic violence of athletes, a Massachusetts study of 107 rapes, attempted rapes, and fondling incidents at 30 national Collegiate Athletic Association (NCAA) Division I schools between 1990-1993 found that male athletes made up 3.3 percent of the male study body at ten of the schools. Those athletes, however, were involved in 10 percent of the assaults (O'Keefe, 1995). Thomas Jackson at the University of Arkansas found that 165 athletes from NCAA programs in the southern United State in 1990, four percent reported physically forcing a date to have sex, 27 percent stated they coerced a woman into sex, and 11 percent reported physically assaulting a woman while on a date. The results were similar to other non-athletic males in college with one difference: when basketball and football players were analyzed separately from other male athletes, they appeared more likely to commit assaults (Burnette, 1996).

Although much of the research on domestic violence does not specifically target a particular group of people, behavior of college students was the focus of this study. The general purpose of the study was to synthesize, apply, and study the abundance of theoretical, clinical, and empirical literature of domestic violence. In addition, the students' participation in athletics was included to study the perceived impact of sports participation on violent behavior.

A survey was conducted using undergraduate students from two state universities in the southeast region of the United States. The same consisted of 835 students from a cross section of academic disciplines and a majority of the students were from low socioeconomic backgrounds within the two universities. The subjects were randomly selected volunteers consisting of both males and females. Each person was asked to complete a 40-item questionnaire that focused on areas such as childhood and family relationships; sexual relationships; family socioeconomic status; experiences in forced sex and fondling; verbal and physical abuse, athletic participation in high school and college; and other forms of violence experienced during and/or before entering college.

During administration of the questionnaire, each subject was assured anonymity and given a short introduction on the purpose of the study. Of the 835 questionnaires received, 759 (91%) were considered useable. Descriptive statistics were obtained on socioeconomic status, marital status, ethnicity, and participation is sports.

Data were obtained from a total of 759 students. Seventy percent were from the lower socioeconomic status and thirty percent were not. Sixty-six percent were females and thirty-four percent were males. The ethnic breakdown included fifty-five percent white, forty percent African-American, and five percent Latin American, Native American, and other ethnic groups that were not identified.

A t-test for independent samples was used to compare perceptions and experiences of violent behaviors between males and females. Several significant differences ($p<.05$) were observed between the student's gender and experiences with violent behaviors. Males reported that family members were more physically aggressive and verbally abusive than females. Also, males reported that they have physically and verbally abused someone of the same sex more often than females. However, females reported having physically abused someone of the opposite sex more often than males while also reporting more verbal abuse from the opposite sex. In addition, males reported being more sexually active than females.

When asked about position of authority, females believed strongly that positions of authority should be shared between males and females. However, males were more likely to endorse the idea that a man should always be the head of the household.

Significant differences between race were also observed. African-American students reported getting along better with family members during the middle school years than did white students. In addition, African-American students were more likely to agree that a man should always be head of the household. However, African-American students were also more agreeable with the idea that females should be in positions of authority than did white students.

The results also indicated a relationship between athletic and non-athletic participation with experiences in violent behavior. Athletes reported less verbal abuse and getting along better with family members than did non-athletes. In addition, athletes reported less physical and verbal abuse by friends and classmates during their K-12 school years than did non-athletes. Finally, athletes were more likely to agree than non-athletes that males should be in positions of authority and heads of households. Although several significant relationships existed between athletes and non-athletes, the number of students that were identified as participants in organized high school or college sports was small. Of the 759 subjects, only 71 (9%) were identified as participants in athletics. Therefore, careful interpretations of the results should be noted.

The results of this study have identified baseline data on domestic violence of college students from low socioeconomic backgrounds. The study has also made an attempt to address some of the issues of violence and its relationship to gender, ethnicity and sports participation. Males are more likely to be physically abused by family members and are more likely to physically and verbally abuse someone of the same sex. However, females reported having physically abused someone of the opposite sex more often than males but also reported more verbal abuse form someone of the opposite sex. African-American students reported getting along better with family members more than white students and athletes reported less verbal and physical abuse from family members and friends than did non-athletes.

The results show that the experiences of domestic violence of college students from low socioeconomic backgrounds are strong indicators that more programs dealing with violent behaviors should be developed on college campuses. Although college officials have no control over the abuse that takes place during the students' early adolescent years, it behooves college administrators and faculty members to address this problem as early as possible through additional research studies and community awareness programs.

References

Bachman, R. (1994). <u>Violence against women</u> Washington, DC: U.S. Department of Justice.

Bandura, A. (1973). <u>Aggression:a social learning analysis</u> Englewood Cliffs, NJ: Prentice Hall.

Burkhart, B. 91996). <u>Acquaintance rape on college campuses</u> Paper Presented at the Rape Prevention on College Campuses Conference In Louisville, KY.

Burnette, E. (1996). Psychologist aims to breed kinder, gentler sportsmen. <u>Monitor,</u> 1.

Butler, E. (1996) Love waits! <u>Valdosta Daily Times</u> p. 2.

Federal Bureau of Investigation (1993). <u>Crime in the United States: Uniform crime reports.</u> Washington, DC: U.S. Government Printing Office.

Jaffee, P. (1986). <u>A guide for health care professionals.</u> State of New Jersey Department of Community Affairs.

Kantrowitz, B. (1993). Wild in the streets. <u>Newsweek,</u> p. 4046.

Moon, B., Trammel-Long, and Vogel, K. (1996). Domestic violence: How Schools can make a difference. <u>The ASCA Counselor, 33,</u> 13.

Myles, B. 91994). Understanding and preventing acts of aggression And Violence in school-age children and youth. <u>Preventing School Failure, 38,</u> (3), 40-46.

Natale, J. (1994). Roots of violence. <u>American School Board Journal, 181,</u> (3), 33-35.

O'Keefee, K. (1995). Domestic abuse has been seen as socially Acceptable. <u>San Antiono Express-News,</u> p. D10.

Rich, J. (1992). Predicting and controlling school violence. <u>Contemporary Education, 64,</u> 35-39.

Salts, C. (1995). Predictive variable of violent behavior in adolescent males. <u>Youth and Society, 26,</u> (3), 377-399.

Schill, K. (1993). Violence among students: schools' liability under section1983. <u>School Law Bulletin, 24</u>, (4), 1-10.

Stephens, R. (1991) Bullies and victims: Protecting our school children. <u>USA Today</u>, p. 4-5.

Zaawitz, M. (1994). <u>Violence between intimates</u>. Washington, DC. U.S. Department of Justice, p. 72-74

CHAPTER 8

Discovering the Potential of the "Whole Child"

Audrey W. Beard, Ed. D.
Albany State University

Melvin A. Shelton, M. Ed.
Albany State University

This chapter demonstrates that all children have learning potential when they are taught through their optimal learning style(s). It reflects relations between several learning styles and teaching styles. This article supports the theory that when students are involved in the learning process, skill mastery will occur and retention of information increases. Picture in your mind the public school classroom, as it was two or three decades ago. Typically, the teacher's desk was at the front of the room and the students' desks were arranged in neat rows. The students' primary tools were textbooks, papers, and pencils. Teachers used chalk boards, overhead projectors, and tape recorders. The primary methods of instruction were teacher presentations to the whole class, teacher-directed instructions, and seatwork. Students were expected to work quietly and on their own most of the school day. Student performance was evaluated with tests and maintained on report cards. Most likely, the classroom behavior management approach was authoritarian, with the teacher in control. Students with learning or behavior problems were instructed in special programs and "pull out" classrooms. Teachers functioned autonomously in their classrooms.

As we enter the 21st century, educators have begun to address the needs of a highly diverse and multicultural student population. Addressing both quality and equity will result in schools that are reformed in ways that will help students from diverse groups to attain academic and social success (Darling-Hammonds, 1992). These are not the best or worse of times, but times of challenge and change. Teachers strive to engage students more actively in learning through instruction that involves discovery, inquiry, and problem solving. Students need teachers who want them to learn, who believe they can learn, and who gives them the kind of experiences that enables them to learn.

The U.S. education system is based on the fundamental belief that all children should be afforded an education, regardless of ethnic background, academic ability, socio-economic status, or geographic location. The task of educating all children is indeed formidable, particularly if we attempt to address the learning needs and styles of a wide diversity of children. In general, scientific interest in learning styles is motivated by the need to discover optional teaching and learning environments that would be sensitive to the unique characteristics of the individual learner. In many areas of the country, heterogeneous classrooms characterized by rich ethnic diversity and varying learning styles have replaced homogeneous classrooms composed of students from similar cultural and ethnic backgrounds. Today about 25% of school age children in the United States are ethnic minorities. By the year 2000, it is estimated that 30% of school age children will be children of color. Projections are that this number will climb to 36% after the year 2001 (Hodgkinson, 1992). A critical question that education must address in the future is: Will white teachers and teachers of color be prepared to address these increasing numbers of culturally diverse students?

The education of the whole child for the twenty-first century is a new and challenging endeavor. The attention of the learning experience has shifted from "art" or "science" to what the child is and what the child needs from the learning environment in order to thrive. All children have the potential to learn, but there is a need for teaching styles/learning styles to tap into that potential. The investigation of learning styles versus teaching styles and multiple intelligence's processes enables one to focus on the child and the "selves": the physical self, the emotional self, the social self, the cognitive self, and the creative self. The impacts of teaching strategies have shown a significant difference in the retention of skill mastery.

The development of the whole child is based on the premises that all selves should be nurtured and is fundamental to the well-being of children. Education must be developmentally appropriate, and children need time to be themselves. If we offer young children we teach rich and appropriate learning opportunities, the childhood will be enhanced, not violated. In the United States, 23% of all children live below the poverty line (Hodgkinson, 1993). Students who are most at risk for not achieving their potential in our schools are children and youth in poverty, regardless of their race. Teachers in the U.S. schools will see increasing numbers of at risk children in their classrooms in the years ahead. Teachers are the heart of the solution. They must understand the dangers associated with stereotyping, especially when the mental images become the basis for educational decisions and also contribute to people being victims of racism (Manning, 1994). Ethnicity should be used to heighten sensitivity to what is valued and taught in particular cultures, rather than relying on generalizations about a culture or race.

In some Hispanic or Spanish - speaking cultures, children are taught that making eye contact with an adult is disrespectful. Korean children out of respect are taught not to look in their teachers' eyes. Vera John (1972) suggests that Navajo children have highly developed visual discrimination and fine motor skills and learn to absorb the world through sight and sounds. Mexican - American students tend to be more field - sensitive. Field sensitive students tend to like to work with others to achieve a common goal. Some Asian-American children are taught to value silence and to avoid overt displays of emotion (Kuriowa, 1975). There is some evidence that learning styles are partially determined by ethnicity and culture (Cole, 1971). Learning styles can be categorized as visual, auditory, or tactile. These cultural differences lead to different socialization practices, which in turn lead to ethnically based differences in how children communicate, learn, and process information (Hale, 1986). Children grow up in distinct culture. Children therefore need an educational system that recognizes their strengths, their abilities, and their culture and that incorporates them into the learning process. Teachers should remind themselves that the student who faces us in a classroom is a unique individual. All students, no matter what their ethnicity, language or family background, have the potential to succeed in school.

One way to address untapped potential in the selves of young children is through the learning style process. Learning style is the way in which each learner begins to concentrate on process, and retain new and difficult information (Dunn & Dunn, 1994). The utilization of the learning style/teaching style method extols the fact that most individuals can learn. One must acknowledge that everyone has strengths, but different people have different strengths.

The learning styles of students and the teaching styles of the teachers are used to develop effective instructional strategies. Most teachers can learn to use learning styles as a cornerstone of their instruction. Dwyer (1991) identifies four domains of instruction at which good teachers excel: (1) content knowledge, (2) teaching for student learning, (3) creating a classroom community for student learning, and (4) teachers professionalism. Villegas (1991) suggests that good teachers in the classroom context incorporates culturally responsive pedagogy, meaning that they adjust their teaching strategies in response to the learning styles of individual students. Learning style teaching recognizes different learning styles and the need for individualized instruction. These challenges will not dissipate, teachers will be called upon to assist directly in developing and implementing educational initiatives to meet these challenges. The teacher will not just be an actor on the stage, he or she must be strategically involved in writing the script.

What happens in school and in the home has a significant effect on the development of the child's natural potential to learn. Successful learning builds self-esteem. The student -teacher interaction is a powerful phenomenon. Thomas Carter's research (1968) into the effects of teachers' expectations on students' learning and classroom behaviors are particularly pertinent. Well-designed and well-implemented learning result in students who function at the upper ranges of the learning scales. Educators in the U.S. schools face the challenge of teaching increasing numbers of children who are culturally and linguistically diverse. Few educators realize that when a person is seated in a hard chair, fully 75 per cent of the total body weight is supported by just 4 square inches of bone (Branton, 1966). The resulting stress on the tissues of the buttock causes fatigue, discomfort, and frequent postural change for which many youngsters are scolded on a daily basis. School experiences, peer attitudes, and teacher expectations directly influence children's performance.

The implementation of technology innovations in education is revolutionizing education, as we know it. The infusion of technology in education has allowed for a refreshing change in the learning process when compared to the traditional lecture and textbook reading as the primary method for learning. Technology in education has opened the gates for new teaching strategies, and caused learning to be more <u>activity</u> oriented. Learning via technology activities provides a vehicle for students to create new knowledge, manipulate data, and stretch their imaginations. This strategy for learning has created an atmosphere in which learners take responsibility for their own learning.

Coupled with this new opportunity for students to learn in new and exciting ways is the opportunity for teachers to provide instruction in many new and different ways. The classroom of today has become a Mecca for hands-on-learning and creative learning activities. Both of these strategies for learning permit the student to become physically involved in maneuvering and controlling models or objects that influence thinking and result in learning. Even the process of directly receiving blocks of information through the Internet is activity oriented. As students participate in learning activities either individually or in groups via computers and multimedia kits, they are assuming more responsibility and they are becoming more responsible for actions that lead to learning. Traditional lecturing and the bland notion of reading page after page in textbooks is becoming obsolete. Learning is invoked through students experimenting with design models and information seeking over the <u>information super highway</u>. Young children use toys for fun and games in the classroom as a strategy for learning. Innovative classroom activities can motivate and inspire a quest for knowledge without the stresses normally associated with classroom learning.

Another learning strategy that all teachers, regardless of subject, are emphasizing is creating a positive image and a strong rapport with students and involving parents in the learning process. Students seem to have greater success at learning in such an environment. Teachers must promote a true sense of caring about students and convey an attitude of genuine interest in the success and well being of students. They should communicate effectively and respect diverse student groups in terms of gender, race, ethnicity, and special needs. The learning curve for students rises significantly when they feel that the instructor is a caring teacher who is sensitive to their needs.

There is a central theme associated with learning strategies and teacher relations that link effective teaching and improved learning. Certainly, it appears that effective communication and a positive relationship with students, combined with learning activities in which students experiment, manipulate, and model objects and data is significant and essential in creating an atmosphere in which students learn best.

Teachers should engage students into the learning process by actively involving students in all activities. Why? Children learn in numerous ways - from reading, observing, listening, talking, and involvement with others. People tend to learn 10% of what they read, 30% of what they see, 50% of what they see and hear; 70% of what they say; 90% of what they say and apply in life, 95% when they teach others (Alcorn, Kinder, & Schunat, 1970). Active learning/involvement in the learning process enables students to participate in authentic activities relevant to real life as modalities are utilized. The modalities may be used as a vehicle for learning, regardless of the learning style, the students, or the teaching style of the teacher. Children learn through their senses best because learning through the senses helps children build (1) visual, (2) auditory, (3) sensory touch (kinesthetic), (4) thermic sense, and (5) olfactory sense. Research suggest that in order to meet the educational needs of "culturally diverse " learners, teachers need to incorporate visual, kinesthetic, and tactile teaching strategies, role playing and sociodramatics teaching strategies, individualized contracts, computer assisted instruction, and one-to-one tutoring. Students may learn by seeing, feeling, tasting, hearing, or smelling an object in a lesson. Which means that regardless of the learning style of the student, every student involved in the activity learns something even if the student only remembers the smell. An example of an activity would be:

How Long Is It?

Objective: To make comparisons of three or more objects that are different lengths.

Materials: Sticks, strips of paper, yarn, drinking straws cut in different lengths, pretzels, tape, tape player.

Activity: A tape with directions on how to compare lengths of masking tape that is taped to a board. Provide students with sticks and other items of different lengths. (2) Let them touch sticks and note different textures (3) Instruct students to look at the different lengths of the objects. (4) Students will then measure the lengths of the objects. (5) Instruct students to place the sticks and other items in order from the shortest to the longest, longest to the shortest. (6) Allow students an opportunity to select different lengths of pretzels to be eaten by the students.

Additionally, other types of activities can be used to accommodate individual learning styles. Examples of other activities utilized could include task cards, matching board games, learning strips, learning circles, electroboards, role playing, cooperative groups, case studies, contracts and multisensory instructional packages. A pedagogy that is responsive to culturally diverse students utilizes their constructed knowledge as a foundation for appropriating new knowledge. Study after study reveals that the teacher is the key to the success or failure of any program, so what you do in your classroom everyday is of primary importance. From the moment students enter the classroom they begin learning. A study was conducted to investigate the instructing practices of public and elementary and secondary teachers in twelve schools in southwest Georgia. The teachers completed 200 surveys. A majority of the teachers answered almost always to addressing learning styles when planning daily activities/lessons. The least number of teachers answered almost always to using television when teaching lessons and using music when teaching all subjects.

It is essential, that all teachers acquire the appropriate attitudes, knowledge, and disposition needed to work effectively with students who come from varied cultural or class backgrounds. Learning style teaching is student-centered rather than teacher-dominated. The teacher plans quality learning activities that engage students in active, hands-on experiences and builds on success to develop students' self-esteem. Emphasizing learning processes is the focus of the utilization of learning style teaching attempts to facilitate learning of every child, assisting each one to reach his or her highest potential. Classrooms must be flexible to allow for the diversity of children being served. When a child has rich, high-quality learning experiences with stimulating activities enhancing his or her development, the effect will likely be lasting.

References

Alcorn, M. D., Kinder, J.S., &Schunert, J. R. (1970). <u>Better teaching in secondary schools</u>. Chicago: Holt, Rinehart and Winston.

Branton (1966) as cited in Dunn, Riter, Dunn, Kenneth, & Perrin, Janet (1994). Teaching

Children Through Their Individual Learning Styles: Practical Approaches for Grades K-2. MA: Allyn and Bacon.

Carter, T.P. (1968). The negative self - concept of Mexican - American student. <u>School and Society</u>, 96, 217 - 219.

Cole, M. (1971). <u>The cultural context of learning and thinking</u>. New York: Basic Book.

Darling-Hammond, L. (1992). Reforming the school reform agenda: New paradigms must restore discourse with local educators. <u>School Administrators,</u> 49(10), 22-27.

Dunn, Riter, Dunn, Kenneth,& Perrin, Janet. (1994). <u>Teaching Children Through Their Individual Learning Styles</u>: Practical Approaches for Grades K - 2. MA: Allyn and Bacon.

Dwyer, C. (1991). Language, culture, and writing (working paper 13). Berkeley, California: Center for the Study of Writing, University of California.

Hodgkinson, H. (1992). <u>A demographic look at tomorrow</u>. Institute for Educational Leadership/Center for Demographic Policy, Washington, D.C.

Hodgkinson, H. (1993). American Education: The good, the bad, and the task. <u>Phi Delta Kappan</u>, 74 (8), 619 - 625.

Hale-Benson, J.E. (1986). Black children: Their roots, cultures, and learning styles (rev.ed.). Baltimore: The John Hopkins University Press.

John, V. P. (1972). Styles of learning –styles of teaching: Reflections on the education

Of Navajo children. In C.B. Cazden, V.P. John, & D. Hymes (Ed.), <u>Functions of</u>

<u>Language in the classroom.</u> New York: Teachers College Press.

Kuroiwa, P. (1975). The invisible student. <u>Momentum</u>. 6, 34-36.

Villegas, A. M. (1991). <u>Culturally responsive pedagogy for the 1990's and beyond</u>. Princeton, N.Y.: Educational Testing Service.

CHAPTER 9

PROVIDING SUPPORT FOR AT-RISK
STUDENTS IN HIGHER EDUCATION

Deborah E. Bembry, Ph.D.
Albany State University
Albany, GA

Sylvia A. Bembry, Ph.D.
Winston-Salem State University
Winston-Salem, NC

Typically, when one discusses at-risk students, the young, school age children come to mind. These children are usually identified by the outward signs of distress and failure such as alcohol and drug abuse, unwed pregnancy, attempted suicide, street crime and delinquency, truancy from school and dropping out; they are defined in terms of demographics or sociological indicators such as family background and socioeconomic status.

Most who work in higher education have been in contact with such students and recognize that at risk is not necessarily related to age, race creed, color, gender, socioeconomic status, etc. Rather, it is a "situation" that prevents any student who has a deficiency from achieving what has been identified as his or her objective. That deficiency may be "suicide level school schedules", unrealistic personal needs and expectations, extreme financial needs, lack of basic academic skills, emotional immaturity, physical limitations or educational or economic background.

Contrary to popular belief, the at-risk student is not a by-produced of the open admissions policies of the 1960's. It can be asserted accurately that bridging the gap between the achievers and non-achievers and persisters versus non-persisters has been a constant in the history of American education and that the controversy surrounding it is an American tradition. Since this is a problem that has persisted over the years it is only logical to assume that it will continue for a life time. The question now becomes, "How do we deal with it?"

Many discussions have been made and many programs have been put in place over the years that have yielded modest results. Project Head Start, Special Education, Chapter I, Vocational Education and Developmental Studies in higher education are but a few examples.

But before we discuss the typical at-risk student as a cultural phenomenon, let's look at another bit of interesting information.. As one reviews the literature one finds an interesting phenomenon: Some at-risk students have a resiliency that sustains them through the tough times and is the key to their success in life. By resiliency, we mean students who stay in school and do well regardless of circumstances. What seems to make the difference? How is it that these students who have been labeled—in essence—failures, become some of the brightest stars and great success stories?

Resilient at-risk students possess temperamental characteristics that elicit positive response from individuals around them (McMillan & Reed 1993). Their personality traits begin in early childhood and are manifested in adolescence as these students seek out new experience and become self-reliant. This begins a cycle of positive reciprocity that enable these students to reach out to other people and expect help. Their positive attitudes are usually rewarded with helpful reactions from those around them. Thus, they come to see the world as a positive place in spite of the difficult issues with which they have to deal. Their positive attitude include respecting others, coming to class prepared, volunteering for in-and out-of-class assignments, and knowing how to "play the school game". High intrinsic motivation and internal locus of control seem to enable resilient at-risk students to succeed.

McMillan and Reed also found that successful resilient students had higher educational aspirations than non-resilient students. These students were motivated by a desire to succeed, to be self starting, and to be personally responsible for their achievements. They attributed poor performance to internal factors such as a lack of effort, not caring, not trying, not studying as much as they needed to, goofing off, and playing around. "These students see themselves as successful because they have chosen to be so and give much credit to themselves." (McMillan & Reed 1993).

So it seems the key to this category of at-risk students is intrinsic motivation. They refused to acknowledge the statistics, the nay sayers and others who doubted their abilities simply based on their skin color, socioeconomic status or gender. For some students a particularly difficult experience, either direct or vicarious, reinforces the importance of getting an education. "Resilient students do not believe that the school neighborhood, or family is critical in either their success or failures. They acknowledge that a poor home environment can make things difficult, but they do not blame their performance on these factors". (McMillan & Reed 1993). Positive thoughts and a belief in themselves seem to have made the difference with these students.(Canfield & Wells 1976).

What about those students who don't have intrinsic motivation or a strong sense of self-efficacy? How do we reach these students? Is it possible? How do we make believers out of these students first and then convince the nay sayers who have labeled and ignored them in the first place?

Institutions that are effective in serving at-risk students are those that respond in particular ways to the students' diverse needs and wants(Compton and Baizerman 1990). Examined from the students' perspective, schools that work are those that ask questions, listen to and hear students, and respond in constructive ways. Effective institutions adapt their responses to students' characteristics and enroll students in programs where there is a suitable match. These institutions continually look for ways to help students succeed. Improving their attrition rate is a by-product of these programs so it puzzles us as to why institutions don't put greater efforts in making adjustments for students.

Perhaps we can learn a lesson or two from resilient students. Teachers play an important role in the success of these students (Geary 1988; Coburn & Nelson 1989; McMillan & Reed l993). Both interpersonal relations and professional competence are important to at-risk students. Students feel that they can talk to "good" teachers and counselors about almost anything. These counselors and teachers "push the students and at the same time are very supportive." (McMillan & Reed 1993).

Finding the Right Match

The management of large class instruction has been and continues to be a part of the academic landscape. This is especially true in the higher education setting. When one adds the dimension of "at risk" students in such an environment, concerns begin to mount. While most accept this method of instruction as the most **efficient** way to meet the needs of the masses, many should and do question whether it is the most **effective** way to meet the needs of individual students. Since this is the situation with most "mainstreamed" students, then certainly one would question whether large group instruction works well with students in at risk situations.

The authors hesitate to use the phrase "at risk" as they feel it is a much overused and maligned term used to separate the "haves" from the "have nots", the minority from the majority and is just one more opportunity to attached still another label to the culturally disenfranchised, educationally deprived and economically disadvantaged. Educators tend to spend so much time labeling and filing away learners that little time and effort is left to assist all students in becoming the best that they can be. To further exasperate the problem, "at risk" is defined differently by different people. As one author put it, "We see 'at risk' through our own ethnic, racial, cultural, and social lenses..."

At one time "at risk" meant minorities—particularly those who came from broken homes or single parent families. At another time, it meant latch key children and children with various physical, mental, intellectual and even social disabilities. They were "properly" labeled, filed and retrieved when summoned by some government agency. Shouldn't we have a common definition of the "problem" before we try to solve it?

Historically black colleges and universities (HBCUs) by their very mission have proven many of these definitions to be in error. When no other institution of higher education would even consider allowing these "at risk" students to attend their college or university, these HBCUs were pulling at risk students up by their boot straps, remediating them when necessary and preparing them to take their rightful place in society. Who would dare say that children of Dr. Martin Luther King are "at risk" because they were raised by a single parent? How about Nikki Giovanni, Oprah Winfrey, James Earl Jones or the many other successful people who must have been labeled "at risk" because of their color or socioeconomic status?

How did they do it? Well, the authors would be just as guilty as those before them if they tried to give credit to one approach or method for these people's success. Rather, there is a recognition of many teaching and learning styles that when properly matched spells success regardless of status. In this day and age of diversity, we dare not overlook this component.

One of these many methods is peer mentoring. In this scenario, large, high risk classes (usually core curriculum) in the humanities, sciences, mathematics and social sciences that have high failure rates are identified. We are all familiar with the large—sometimes 200-500 students—cost effective classrooms usually associated with the college landscape. We remember being thrust in to such a situation in graduate school after having experienced relatively small classes at a small (2000+) college. After a few weeks of culture shock, our resiliency kicked in and as a result, we are the success story you are reading about now. How did we do it? We organized ourselves. We went to class each time it met. We prepared before we went to class and reviewed after we left class. Class assignments were taken care of immediately, rather than at the last minute or even worse, after the due date. We prepared for tests by reading everything we could get our hands on rather than asking the teacher the day before, do we need to know this for the test. We participated in class discussions, debates and volunteered for other activities. We anticipated questions, prepared and took mock examinations often. We sat up front (when there were no seating charts) and were attentive and appeared to be interested even if we were not. In other words, we became model students.

Thus, the peer mentoring model is certainly one possibility to help at-risk students who are placed in an environment designed for failure. Once the high risk classes are identified, the real work begins. Students who have already taken these classes and were successful (made an "A" or "B") are identified and challenged to serve as "models" of good student behavior. These "expert students" or models are then paired with a professor who teaches a large class as his/her assistant. Now we have the potential for success.

While there is an assumption that these model students knew what it took to be successful in these particular courses, they should be taught or reminded how to be model students. Once the students accept the challenge, they are hired and given charges that include attending classes daily, participating in workshops for study skills, time management and the like. Additionally, they must attend high enrollment classes and serve as role models by taking notes, stimulating discussions, asking questions and holding study sessions for fellow classmates at least twice a week.

Pairing these at risk students with peer mentors can go a long way in improving academic success as well as social and emotional development. They work with people who are similar ages, have similar backgrounds and interest. They are more likely to be inspired because these students" did it" and so can I. As these at- risk students become involved in the study skills sessions hey not only have a mentor they can rely on but the opportunity to form small study groups develop. Sometimes life long friendships are made through these contacts.

With such a program, an institution accomplishes several goals. Four of them include saving on financial resources by using student assistants instead of hiring another salaried professor, giving students opportunities to demonstrate their leadership and teaching skills and most importantly, improving students' performance in core courses and the institution's retention rate..

Since students will be completing their core requirements during their first two years of higher education, this is the ideal time to get them off to a good start. If they establish good habits from the beginning, they will do better academically and otherwise. If students are successful academically, they are more likely to complete their education and become productive citizens. The more productive citizens there are, the less "at risk" situations in which children can be placed. Thus, the society will be well on it's way of producing a literate citizenry void of non productive labels.

REFERENCES

Canfield, J., and H. C. Wells. 1976. 100 Ways to Enhance Self-Concept in the Classroom, Englewood Cliffs, New Jersey: Prentice Hall, Inc.

Coburn, J. & S. Nelson. 1989. Teachers do make a difference: What Indian graduates say about their school experience (Report No. RC-017-103). Washington, D. C.: Office of Educational Research and Improvement. (ERIC document Reproduction Service No. ED 306 071)

Compton, d. & M. Baizerman. 1990. "Services for At-Risk Students in Schools." Children Today. July/August, pp. 8-10.

Geary, P. A. 1988. "Defying the odds?": Academic Success Among at-risk Minority Teenagers in an Urban High School (Report No.UD-026-258). Paper presented at the annual meeting of the American Educational research Association, New Orleans, LA. (ERIC Document Reproduction Service No. ED 296 055)

Jenkins, J. R. and L. Jenkins. 1987 "Making Peer Tutoring Work," Educational Leadership, vol. 44, p. 6, March.

McMillan, J. H & D. F. Reed. 1993. A Qualitative Study of Resilient At-Risk Students. Paper presented at the1993 annual meeting of the American Educational Research Association, Atlanta.

Ogden, Evelyn Hunt, and Vita Germinario 1988 The At-Risk Student Answers for Educators, Lancaster, Pennsylvania, Technomic Publishing Co. Inc.

Walter, L. M. 1984. "Life line to the Underprepared". Improving College and University Teaching. Vol. 30, No. 4, pp. 159-160.

Chapter 10
Configuring Curriculum in low socioeconomic schools for increasing student Achievement

Burel Block Ph.D.
Albany State University

Curriculum that augments the probability of increasing student standardized achievement test scores will be both written and practiced differently than currently practiced in low socioeconomic schools. Curriculum should be both challenging and interesting to both teacher and students. Principals as instructional leaders must search out teachers with strong verbal ability. They must secure more teachers per pupil, more teachers with higher degrees, and teachers with more experience and tenure. These teachers need to take the initiative to create school discipline plans that categorize what principals are to handle and what teachers are expected to handle (Ferguson, 1991).

Principals often require teachers to spend inordinate amounts of time decorating their classrooms. They do this at the expense of planning for the next day's lessons for reading, writing, and arithmetic. They spend hours decorating for Halloween, Thanksgiving, Christmas, New Years, and Easter. As if that is not enough they spend even more time decorating for Washington's, Lincoln's, King's, and Chief John Ross' birthdays. Essentially the curriculum is coloring, pasting, and posting because that is what their teachers do most of the time.

If all bulletin boards were removed from some 80,000 American schools, achievement test scores would probably double the first year.

Not only are teachers spending inordinate amounts of time decorating, coloring, pasting, and posting, their students are also doing it first. Secondly, teachers see their students' sloppy work then decide to do it all over again themselves.

If teachers don't change decorations after each great event, the misguided principal will direct them to, under the threat of insubordination, if they don't do it. So instead of being engaged in preparing science labs for instruction, which consumes a great deal of time and work, teachers are gleefully coloring, pasting, and posting with their pupils (Pupil indicates a child is present while a student is one who studies and learns). The key to success in any school organization, rich or poor, is instructional leadership: the school principal (Deck, Nov. 18, 1998).

When teachers hear the word, "curriculum" connotations of reams of paperwork are conjured up. Images of hours of committee meetings, hours of planning and curricular guides that generally will never be used. The American managerial philosophy of management from the top down to the bottom burns up a lot of teachers' time and frees curriculum directors to conjure up even more ways to waste teachers' time. Thus is created a-keep-'em-busy cycle that produces little or no increase in student achievement test scores.

The Curriculum Director

Instead of each teacher writing daily lesson plans, the curriculum director should write them. (At the very least it would keep them busy). Teachers often don't even know what the curricular objectives are, nor do they know what they mean. The curriculum director is the specialist; therefore, the curriculum director should write lesson plans and give them to the classroom teachers to follow. That's what one Japanese school did (Block, 1992).

If curriculum directors wrote daily lesson plans for all teachers, teachers would be freed to spend more time preparing activities to accomplish those plans. The curriculum director could easily see that the curriculum was aligned with achievement test objectives and various state curricular objectives. This one policy change would change the hit-or-miss curricular planning practiced in public schools today.

Teachers do not object to being told what to teach because they are already told what to teach by various agencies: state school boards and local school boards. Teachers would still be at liberty to determine the best strategies, tactics, and techniques in which to present the material. Curriculum directors may offer alternative strategies, tactics, and techniques from which teachers may choose.

Curricular Goals

Goal setting and motivation research generates intense interest in the education community (Jewell and Siegall, 1990). Research makes it clear that goal-setting works. Current research is more interested in why it works, than if it does (So.., they find out why it works then it stops working?). There are five important features to goal setting:

1. The goal works better if it is specific. Koch (1979) revealed that specific goals aided understanding that increased the probability goals would be achieved. Tubbs (1986) found that specific goal setting produced results.
2. The difficulty of the goal should be perceived as moderate to high. Goals that are perceived as too easy generally suffer a credibility loss. Latham, Mitchell, and Dossett (1978) found employee participation in goal setting led to higher goals being set. There was a linear relationship between goal difficulty and performance.
3. Persons responsible must accept the goals. They must agree to achieve them. They should believe in the feasibility of goal achievement. Goal commitment is influenced by authority, peer influence, rewards, costs, competition, cooperation, and believability (Locke, Latham, & Erez, 1988).
4. Feedback makes a difference in progress toward accomplishing goals. Feedback may be built into the goal. It may come from the school principal, or the teacher may provide it, or the students themselves can provide the necessary feedback. It encourages, reinforces, and corrects (Ivancevich and McMahon, 1982).
5. Participative goal setting helps the achiever to better understand what is

expected. Better understanding increases the probability that the goal will be achieved. More difficult goals generally produce higher performance. No significant difference was found in participative- and assigned-goal setting (Latham, Mitchell, and Dossett, 1978).

Research shows that goal development does not need faculty input; however, it is essential that the faculty be well informed as to what the goals are (Jewell & Siegall, 1990). The curriculum director should establish curricular goals and objectives that are aligned with the standardized achievement tests. Then the director should administer short exams that sample the progress of students on attaining the established curricular goals. The curriculum director should design, administer, and score sampling examinations. Since time is a prime classroom commodity, sampling exams should not take more than 30 minutes to administer about every two weeks.

Once sampling exams are scored and the data are summarized by school, by classroom, and by student, the summary scores should be charted and publicly displayed. School and classroom charts should be displayed so that everyone in the school is aware of the school's progress on the curricular goals. Individual students' progress should be shared with teachers, students, and parents (Jewell & Seigall, 1990)

Goals for Improving Test Scores:

1. Secure a list of the achievement test objectives for reading, math, science, and social studies.
2. Align the curriculum with the achievement test objectives.
3. Develop a feedback/monitoring calendar.
4. Design and implement a reward system for positive progress.
5. Design activities to emphasize the importance of achievement test scores to student and to teachers.

Goal I: Secure Achievement test objectives.

A. Activities:

1. Ask the coordinator of district testing for a copy for each test objective for each subject area.
2. Distribute test objectives to each teacher.
3. Distribute test objectives to parents and students.

B. Resources for support:

1. Paper
2. Copies
3. Time

C. Expected outcomes resulting from the completion of activities

1. Teachers and students will be informed.
2. There will be a positive direction for the curriculum.

Goal II: Align the curriculum with achievement test objectives.

A. Activities designed to accomplish this goal:

1. Develop a curricular calendar for teaching achievement test objectives once every two weeks before the achievement test is given.
2. Develop a curricular calendar for each subject area.

B. Resources to support activities:

1. Budgeted class time.
2. Specific computer programs that address achievement test objectives.
3. Specifically assigned homework.

C. Expected outcomes:

1. Achievement test scores will increase five or more percent.
2. Teachers, students, and parents will be informed.

Goal III: Feedback Calendar.

A. Activities designed to accomplish goals:

1. Design curriculum director-made tests for measuring progress on each achievement test objective.
2. Give the curriculum director-made tests every two weeks by subject area.
3. Chart the progress of each grade level in each school on the achievement test objectives by subject area.
4. Post attractive trend-line charts in each school.

B. Resources to support activities:

1. Time for the curriculum director to design tests.
2. Chart paper and supplies.
3. Time for curriculum director to grade tests.

C. Expected outcomes resulting from the completion of activities:

1. Increased awareness of progress.
2. Establishment that the achievements test is important.
3. A cooperative spirit to improve.

Goal IV: Develop a reward system

A. Activities designed to accomplish goals:

1. Reward students when the class shows progress on the trend-line charts, special recess, parties, ice cream socials, principal?s recognition of class, etc.
2. Give the class showing the most progress special privileges, e.g., first to lunch or recess.

B. Resources to support activities:

1. A calendar of activities.
2. Principal's support
3. Treats

C. Outcomes:

—

116

1. Students will feel positive about working and studying.
2. Students will enjoy the friendly cooperative learning.
3. Students will score higher on the achievement test.

Goal: V. Design activities to emphasize the importance of achievement test scores to student and to teachers.

A. Activities designed to accomplish goal:
1. Design a calendar to periodically discuss the importance of standardized testing in an industrialized society.
2. Teachers should discuss the importance of scoring well on standardized achievement tests, e.g., SAT, MAT, MCAT, LSAT, GRE, etc.

B. Resources to support activities:
1. Teachers budget time to develop a discussion for students.
2. Teachers budget time for research.
3. Handouts

C. Outcomes:
1. Students will understand the importance of standardized testing in an industrial society.
2. Students will feel positive about working and studying.
3. Students will enjoy friendly cooperative learning.
4. Students will score higher on achievement tests.

Science instead of fiction: "The truth shall make you free." John 8:32

The Lord taught the truth. Public school teaches fiction. Sixty percent of class time in American public elementary schools is spend teaching the reading of fiction (Whinny the Pooh Pooh). Five percent of the school week is spent teaching science, the truth. If achievement test scores are to increase significantly, then more time must be spent studying science in elementary schools. Preferable at least sixty minutes daily should be spent studying laboratory science. Children who can read reading as currently taught cannot always read science; however, children who can read science can invariably read reading.

The governing variable that drives the teaching of fiction in American schools is the large percent of female elementary teachers. Women generally have math and science phobias; consequently, they steer the daily lessons away from science and math toward fiction because in fiction if one does not know, one just makes it up as one goes along. Science teachers must know science that makes them constant students.

Children begin school by studying reading with a content that is mostly fiction. America's competitive ability in the free market place depends on knowledge of science not fiction. Children who generally can read the materials in reading cannot necessarily read the materials in science; however, those children who can read science can read both science and reading. An added bonus, i.e., for expertise in reading science, students also develop expertise in mathematics. Science, the one subject with three pedagogical benefits, is usually taught only minimally in American elementary schools.

If one desires to increase students' standardized achievement test scores in low socioeconomic schools, one good strategy would be to increase the number of minutes spent on reading and studying science. Science concentrates on the real world that possesses the most fascinating subjects for children to discover through the scientific method. Measuring, evaluating, analyzing, categorizing, and observing the real world makes the study of mathematics concrete and sensible. Since English is laden with many Latin derivatives, students who spend more time studying science are learning more Latin derived linguistic concepts which they will employ even more in the future when they enroll in college.

The American curricular sequence is neurologically turned upside down. We wait until high school to begin the study of foreign language. Children two and three years of age are much more capable and much more equipped for learning language than at any other time of their lives. Foreign language studies should begin in pre-kindergarten or earlier. It should be taught daily every year until high school graduation. With the increasing easy of travel and telecommunications, it has become increasingly more imperative that all Americans be bilingual at least. The study of foreign language not only opens up more avenues of communication, but it also increases the neuroplastic capacity of the student.

Curriculum should be based on the following two concepts: (a) "If ye have faith as a grain of mustard seed...nothing shall be impossible into you" (Matthew 17:20). (b) "We begin with the hypothesis that any subject can be taught effectively in some intellectually honest form to any child at any stage of development (Bruner, 1960 p. 33)." Both teachers and parents should practice believing that children can learn all things. The only quantitative limits of the brain's ability to learn are the amounts of available time and the richness of the environment. Consequently, only time and geography limit the healthy child.

Perseverance should be emphasized and made important to students continually and redundantly. One of the main reasons that Japanese education has been so successful is the effectiveness of teaching perseverance (gambaru) by both parents and teachers. Perseverance is one of the major tenets of most major religions. It is a great teaching of both Christianity and Buddhism.

Mental discipline does work. You can learn anything you want, just as long as you work hard enough. The Japanese accept this maximum in total faith. Some American educators proclaim that one must be gifted genetically before any significant learning can take place. We begin categorizing children right away into ready and unready learning groups. Then we group them by at-risk, gifted, learning disabled, regular learners, and accelerated learners. Such labeling officially sets and consequently lowers expectations of what children can learn.

Thorndike maintained that the mere cognitive process of mathematics helped strengthen the learning process (Modern neuroscience supports his hypothesis). The brain was viewed as a muscle that if exercised it would become stronger and more efficient. He deducted this from watching his cats grow smarter. (I believe he would have had better luck with dogs.) Subsequently, American educators concluded that mental discipline did not work. They proposed higher level thinking. Seems some excellent ideas were being spawned in the shuttle and at high altitudes. They concluded that the hyperspace between the motor cortex and the upper skull was the place learning really occurred.

What is higher level thinking? After thirty years of research the author concludes it is thinking so fashioned that only the thinker can understand it. It may be that a tall person has higher level thinking than a short one? Or an airline pilot has higher level thinking than say a sailor?

Back to perseverance, the Japanese taught their children "Kaizen" a constant quest for perfection. *Kaizen* pervades the personal philosophies of Asians (Peters, 1987). Davis (1991) wrote that the Koreans were fiercely determined to succeed in all attempts. It is little wonder then that their children out score ours on achievement test scores.

Compressed Curriculum

A greater number of better-educated high school students enrolled in college will upgrade the challenges facing currently enrolled college students. Compared to Japanese and German high schools our high school curriculum is more on the level with their elementary curriculum. The next logical step is to compress our curriculum downward, teaching more secondary courses at the elementary levels, and more college courses at the secondary level, and more graduate courses at the under graduate level.

Policy on Reading

"This search for a meaning to one's existence is man's most primary concern" (Frankl, 1959, p. 97). The key to learning is meaning and understanding. Meaning is the primary precept of the Whole Language Reading Program. Universities in states with high achievement test scores train elementary teachers to teach reading by using the Whole Language technique. Whole Language classrooms have students write every day. Whole Language operates under the assumption that language is acquired through purposeful use (Heald-Taylor, 1989). In New Zealand, children start to school on their fifth birthday. By utilizing a Whole Language Program they start reading and writing immediately in their first year of school. That a child can read what the child speaks and writes is a major assumption of Whole Language theory (Cambourne, 1988). Three-year-old children have developed an already complex language hence they should be able to read what they are speaking and writing. Children acquire the spoken language naturally (Slobin, 1985) consequently, children should acquire reading naturally if given the proper conditions. The child's recorded language has been used effectively to teach reading (Van Allen and Van Allen, 1982; Stauffer, 1970).

Eighty percent of intelligence is developed by age eight. Children learn the quickest and the greatest quantity of information from one to five years of age (Bloom, 1964). When teachers improve their strategies for teaching reading at earlier ages, children will come to the first grade with better-developed neuroplasticity (Healy, 1991). Such would liberate teachers to spend more time teaching science, math, and higher levels of thinking.

Moir and Jessel (1991) indicated a physical difference in the brains of boys and girls. The masculine brain is more attuned to spatial orientation. While the feminine brain is more attuned to auditor orientations. If this were true then boys should learn to read more quickly through immediate visual stimuli and girls more quickly with auditory stimuli.

Some elementary schools refuse to let their students take home their new reading books. It was with a great deal of sadness that teachers were told it was against state law for children to take their new reading books home and that they had to keep them in the classroom. From my experience in Minnesota which ranked third in the nation in reading scores, children who have the right to read their new readers at home with their parents score better.

Well, an even better idea would be for schools to require children to purchase their new readers at cost, or even a little less than cost. It would save the state money by reducing the amount of time needed to maintain books on inventory for seven or eight years. The advantage would be the great opportunity to teach children the responsibility of private ownership and the pride of owning one's very own reading book. Such a policy would put books in homes that are presently dominated by television.

Reading is best learned through writing. If one can write it one can generally read what one wrote. The thumb and fingers have a very large neuroplastic representation in the somatosensory cortex of the brain (Kandel & Hawkins Sept. 1992). Writing requires one to recall what was read. In the act of recall choline is consumed which indicates the consequence of learning (Chafetz, 1990). Primary students should spend great quantities of time writing. They should read and write for a purpose. Writing letters to parents, mayors, governors, principals, and teachers that discuss issues of concern are productive ways to teach reading.

For those first graders who have difficulty learning to read, the school should employ programs similar to Reading Recovery in which intensive individualized tutoring in reading by trained teachers is utilized to teach reading. No student should have to leave the first grade without the skill of reading. Reading Recovery has proven to be one of the most effective programs for helping the troubled first grade reader to learn how to read.

Reading Recovery can practically eliminate the special education classification of learning disability (LD). In the 1977-87 decade approximately 20,000 to 80,000 U.S. children were inaccurately labeled LD because they actually possessed normal patterns of reading growth. By decreasing class size for grades K-3 to 15 children per teacher or less and by adding teacher-tutors, America would effectively reduce the overall cost of education while improving quality.

To recap if children have trouble learning to read and write when they start their second year at age six, they are placed in a program called Reading Recovery.

Reading Recovery provides intensive; one-to-one individually designed lessons for 30 minutes each day. Children read many little books, write, and read short passages. Every day the child is introduced to a new book that he (mostly boys) will read independently the next day. The child continues in the program until he has developed effective strategies for independent learning that permits him to be successful in the regular classroom. Primary Education

More resources must be channeled to the primary grades if there is to be significant change in the quality of public education. Teachers in kindergarten to third grades should never be assigned more than 15 children (A classroom instructional aide is not a teacher). Children should never be labeled learning disabled, behaviorally disturbed, emotionally disturbed, or learning deficit. Children should never be held back in kindergarten, first, second, or third grades. Children should be taught in a manner in which reading makes sense. Children should never be grouped by ability. Children should be taught to believe if they work hard enough they will learn. Presently states, parents, and educators practice all the above detrimentally to children.

More secondary subjects need to be brought down to the primary school. Wood working, mechanics, foreign language, algebra, physics, chemistry, biology, home economics, piano, and dance. Wood working and science labs should be ergonomically designed to accommodate the primary student. Wood working serves as an excellent vehicle for teaching math and the process of creativity. Mechanics could be taught through small engine repair that would give teachers the opportunity to teach the concepts of physics in a practical and realistic format. Such hands-on experience would accelerate learning. When students write about wood working projects and the repair of lawn mower engines it would intensify the interest of boys in academics.

Foreign language is best learned by primary children who generally possess more eidetic memory until after puberty. At such time memory tends to become more linear and less photographic (Rose, 1992).

Primary education must receive first priority in the budget if there is to be significant reform. Reform calls for primary class sizes (K-3) to be reduced to no more than 15 children per teacher. Our best teachers should be assigned to primary grades. We should make sure that every primary child has the opportunity to choose the best available books to read and that each one has an opportunity to interact with a well-educated teacher every day. Most of our education dollars should go to primary education not to secondary education. It is too late by that time to make any great changes. An 80% return on the education dollar at the primary level will make a much greater impact on SAT than an 8% at the secondary level.

Formal instruction should begin as early as two years of age if one wishes to maximize a child's potential to learn. Earlier instruction will better prepare children for the academic world of school. Naturally the better prepared children are before the first grade, the greater will be the increase in student standardized achievement test scores.

Middle School and High School

Middle school and high school should have curriculum that is dominated by science. Since many students take the PSAT, SAT, or ACT, then they should all be enrolled in science, math, and foreign language each year of the six years they are in secondary school. English, social studies, and literature should be combined in one course that is dominated by writing. If student achievement test scores are to be significantly increased, then the secondary curriculum must be significantly restructured in alignment with the standardized achievement tests.

The investment with the greatest return.

Nine year old children have learned 50% of what they will learn by high school graduation (Bloom, 1964). Children learn more with teachers who teach no more than 15 children in kindergarten through third grade (Robinson & Wittebols, 1986). Children learn more when they are not labeled learning disabled, behaviorally disabled, emotionally disabled, hyperactive, or attention deficit (Kelly,

1978). Children learn more when they are not retained in transitional first grades (Shepard & Smith, 1989). Children learn more when reading is taught by the Whole Language method (Krashen, 1982 & Slobin, 1979). Children learn more when they are not grouped by ability (Biehler & Snowman, 1986). Children learn more if they believe work is more important than talent or giftedness (White, 1987). Psychoneurological

Existing research calls for significant restructuring at the primary school level. Psychoneurological findings call for curriculum to be designed by gender. To accelerate the learning of both boys and girls curriculum must be tailored to match their interests and neurophysiology: more math, science, and biography for primary boys; more verbalization for girls in math (Moir & Jessel, 1991). Neuroplasticity

Neuroplasticity requires that children receive a quality experiential education from birth to puberty. More resources must be made available at conception to nine years of age. The formative years are much more a determinant of future academic success than any other period in a child's academic life.

Summary

Schools in low socioeconomic communities should seek out principals who are strong instructional leaders. Such principals must lead teachers to develop effective discipline plans. They should employ the most articulate teachers they can find. They need to hire more teachers with graduate degree and with more experience per pupil. They need to assure that classroom teachers spend more time on instruction and less on paperwork. They need to involve their curriculum directors more in preparing lesson plans for teachers. They need to spend more quality time on setting goals and the teaching of science and math. They need to increase their expectations for what students are capable of achieving. They need to spend more time teaching children to persevere. They need to provide more significant meaning to what children are reading. Finally, they need to expect children to learn more at earlier ages.

References

Block, B. (1992). Izu San: The elementary school in Atami, Japan, (video) Albany State College, 1992

Bloom, B. S. Stability and change in human characteristics. John Wiley & Sons, Inc.: New York, 1964.

Berlyne, D.E. (1958). The influence of the albedo and complexity of stimuli on visual fixation in the human infant. The BritishJournal of Psychology. 49, 315-318.

Bruner, J. S. (1960). The process of education. New York: Vintage Books.

Cambourne, Brian. (1988). The whole story. New York: Ashton Scholastic.

Chafetz, M. D. (1990). Nutrition and neurotransmitters: the nutrient bases of behavior. Englewood Cliffs, New Jersey: Prentice Hall.

Davis, Jr., B. O. (1991). Benjamin O. Davis, Jr. American. Washington: Smithsonian Institution Press.

Deck, L. (Nov. 18, 1998). Three simple truths about leadership. Leadership News, 7(1): 8.

Ferguson, R.F. (1991). Paying for public education: new evidence on how and why money matters. Harvard Journal on Legislation, 28, 465-498.

Frankl, V. E. (1959). From death-camp to existentialism. Boston: Beacon Press.

Heald-Taylor, Gail. (1989). The administrator's guide to whole language. New York: Owen Publishers, Inc.

Healy, J. M. (1990). Endangered minds: Why our children don?t think. New York: Simon and Schuster.

Hunter, M., Ames, D. & Koopman, R. (1983). Effects of stimulus complexity and familiarization time on infant preferences for novel and familiar stimuli. Developmental Psychology, 19, 338-352.

Ivancevich, J. M., and McMahon, J.T. (1982). The effects of goal setting, external feedback, and self-generated feedback on outcome variables: A field experiment. Academy of management journal, 25:359-372.

Jewell, L.N. and Siegall, M. (1990). Contemporary Industrial/Organizational Psychology. New York: West Publishing Co.

Kandel E. R. & Hawkins, R. D. (Sept. 1992). The biological basis of learning and individuality. Scientific American, 267(3), 53(8)

Koch, J.L. (1979). Effects of goal specificity and performance feedback to work groups on peer leadership, performance, and attitudes. Human relations, 32:819-840.

Latham, G.P., Mitchell, T.R. and Dossett, D.L. (1978). Importance of participative goal setting and anticipated rewards on goal difficulty and job performance. Journal of applied psychology, 63:163-171.

Locke, E.A. (1968). Toward a theory of task motivation and incentives. Organizational behavior and human performance, 3:157-189.

Locke, E.A., Latham, G.P., and Erez, M. (1988). The determinants of goal commitment. Academy of management review, 13:23-39.

Locke, E.A., Shaw, K.N., Saari, L.M., and Latham, G.P. (1981). Goal setting and task performance: 1969-1980. Psychological bulletin, 90:125-152.

Lowenfeld, B. (1927). Systematisches Studium der Reaktionen der Sauglinge auf Klange und Gerausche. Z. Psychol., Abt. 1, 104, 62-96.

Moir, A. & Jessel, D. (1991). Brain sex. New York: Carol Publishing Group.

Peters, T. (1987). Thriving on Chaos. New York: Harper & Row.

Piaget, J. (1936). La Naissance de l'intelligence chez l'enfant. Delachaux & Niestle, Neuchatel & Paris. (The Orignis of Intelligence in Children. New York: International Universities Press, 1952).

Robinson, G. E. and Wittebols, J. H. (1986). Class size research: a related cluster analysis for decision making. Arlington: Educational Research Service, Inc.

Rose, S. (1992). The making of memory. New York: Doubleday.

Shepard, L. A. & Smith, M. L. (1989). Flunking Grades. New York: Falmer Press.

Slobin, D. I. (1979). Psycholinguistics. Dallas: Scott, Foresman and Co.

Slobin, D. (1985). The cross-linguistic study of language acquisition. Nillsdale, N.J.: Erlbaum.

Staples, R. (1932). The response of infants to colors. Journal of Exp. Psychology. 15, 119-141.

Stauffer, R. G. (1970). The language experience approach to the teaching of reading. New York: Harper & Row.

Tubbs, M.E. (1986). Goal setting: A meta-analytic examination of the empirical evidence. Journal of applied psychology, 71:474-483.

Van Allen, R. and Van Allen, C. (1982). Language experience activities. Boston, MA: Houghton Mifflin.

Voss, H. G. & Keller, H. (1983). Curiosity and exploration: theories and results. New York: Academic Press.

Yatsevitch, M. (1988). Reading with the troubled reader. Portsmouth: Heinemann.

Chapter 11

Instructional Strategies for Teachers Who Teach Children Who are Victims of Poverty.

Claude Perkins, Ph.D.
Albany State University

Roslind Growe, Ph.D.
University of Southwestern Louisiana

Alice Duhon-Ross Ph.D
Albany State University

The pervasive practices in classrooms across America were many teachers assume students arrive to school ready to learn regardless of the circumstances they are subjected to prior to arriving at the school. Concurrent with this assumption, many feel all children have the same learning modality. Even though many educators have widely argued that school systems, school programs, organizational and structural features of school, and the school environment contribute to the conditions that influence student's academic failure (Boyd, 1991;Cuban, 1989, Waxman, 1992). These assumptions continue to persist. The school environment is the broader context or climate of the school can either facilitate or constrain classroom instruction and student learning Shields, 1991).
Such constraints can create an at risk school environment that (a) alienate students and teachers, (b) provide low standards and low quality of education, (c) have differential expectations for students, (d) have high non-completion rates for students, (e) are unresponsive to students, (f) have non-completions rates for students, (g) are unresponsive to students, (h) have dsciplinary problems, or (i) do not adequately prepare students for the futre (Waxman, 1992). Children who are victims of poverty who attend schools in at risk environmental situations deserve special attention if they are going to experience success. Thus we must alter their learning environment, in order to improve both their education and their overall chances for success in society.

Several studies have documented the problems associated with classroom instruction for minority students and students in at risk situations. These studies, for example, have found hat some teachers provide differential treatment for some types of students as compared to others (Babad, 1990, 1993). In particular, studies have found that teachers praise and encourage minority students less often that their white classmates and that teachers sometimes have lower expectations for minority and disadvantage students than their white classmates (Lucas & Schecter, 1992; Smey Richman, 1989) In addition, several studies have found that schools serving disadvantaged or lower achieving students often devote less time and emphasis to higher order thinking skills than do schools serving more advantaged students (Allington & McGill-Franzen, 1989; Coley & Hoffen, 1990; Padron & Waxon, 1993). Lower achieving and minority students have often been denied the opportunity to learn higher level thinking skills because it has been believed that the must demonstrate the ability to learn the basics or lower levels of knowledge before they can be taught higher level skills (Foster, 1989; Means & Knapp, 1991). Furthermore, there is generally an emphasis on remediation for low achievers, which has resulted in teacher's lower expectations and a less-challenging curriculum for these students as well as an overemphasis on repetition of content through drill and practice (Knapp & Schields, 1990; Lehr & Harris, 1988). The result of these practices may lead to students adopting behaviors of learned helplessness and having a passive orientation to schooling (Coley & Hoffman, 1990). These pedagogically induced learning problems or instructional inadequacies may also account for student's poor academic achievement and low motivation (Fletcher & Cordona-Morales, 1990).

In urban schools, the most common instructional approach is the direct instructional model where teachers typically teach to the whole class at the same time and control all of the classroom discussion and decision making (Bookhart & Rusnak, 1993; Haberman, 1991; Padron & Waxman, 1998). This teacher-directed instructional model emphasizes lecture, drill and -practice, remediation, and student seatwork consisting mainly of worksheets (Stephen, Varble, & Taitt,

1993). Haberman (1991) argues that this over reliance on direct instruction in urban schools constitutes a "pedagogy of poverty" if no other methodologies are employed. He maintains that this teacher-directed, instructional style leads to student compliance and passive resentment as well as teacher burn out. Furthermore, he criticizes this orientation because teachers are generally held accountable for "making" students learn, while students usually assume a passive role with low engagement in task or activities that are generally not authentic.

Many educators and policy maker are calling for changing models of teaching and learning that emphasize more active student learning (Sheingold, 1990) and changing the role of teachers from a deliverer of knowledge to one of a facilitator of learning (Wiburg, 1991). The following three approaches stress this changing model of classroom instruction and they all have been found to be previously successful for students at risk of failure in urban schools. These research-based instructional approaches are: (a) cognitively guided instruction, (b) critical/responsive teaching, and (c) technology use. The following will briefly describe each of these approaches explaining why they may especially successful for student who are victims of poverty.

Cognitively Guided Instruction

Influenced by theory and research form the filed of cognitive psychology, many educators have adopted an information processing view of learning and teaching (Shuell, 1993). From this perspective, learning is viewed as an active porches and teaching as a means of facilitating active student mental processing (Gagne, 1985) This cognitive approach a suggest that students need to apply cognitive strategies in order to learn, (Winne, 1985). Therefore, cognitively guided instruction emphasizes the development of students' cognitive learning strategies as well as techniques and approaches that foster students' metacognition and cognitive monitoring of their own learning (Irvin, 1992; Linn & Songert, 1991; Pressley & Ghatala, 1990; Waxman et al.,). From an instructional perspective, this approach requires that teachers need to focus on affective, motivational, metacognitive, developmental, and social factors that influence students since they all occur simultaneously and are all critical to students' learning (Presidential Task Force on Psychology in Education. 1993).

This instructional approach can be very beneficial for the large number of students who are not doing well in school because once students learn how to effectively use cognitive strategies, some of the individual barriers to academic success faced by this group may be remove. In reading, for example, low-achieving students have been found to use different reading strategies and fewer strategies than high-achieving students (Padron, Kniht, & Waxman, 1986). Unless more is learned about the strategies used by academically disadvantaged students in comprehending text and how to effectively instruct them in reading, these students may experience serious academic problem in school (Stien, Leinhardt, & Bickel, 1989)

Critical/Responsive Teaching

In schools today, there is a mismatch between what schools are emphasizing and the needs and concerns of students (Gordon & Yowell, 1994). In addition to providing students who are victims of poverty with cognitively guided instruction, there is also a need to provide these students with critical or responsive teaching. Responsive teaching addresses the mismatch between what the goals and mission of schooling and student's current needs and concerns. It also addresses the serious miscommunication problems that can occur in classrooms when teachers do not understand their students' social and cultural milieu (Lucas & Schecter, 1992). Responsive teaching focuses on the students needs and cultural and tries to create conditions that supports the empowerment of students (Darder, 1993).

This type of pedagogues is often called "culturally-sensitive instruction" (Boyer, 1993), or multicultural instruction" (Saldana & Waxman, 1994) and it focuses on the everyday concerns of students and tries to incorporate these concerns into the curriculum. It requires a learner-centered instructional approach, where teachers assume the role of a facilitator rather than the source of all knowledge (Bracnh,

Goodwin, & Gualtieri, 1993). Critical/responsive teaching, however, is more than merely including aspects of the student' cultures into the curriculum, textbooks, and learning activities. It also focuses on the critical family and community issues that students encounter daily. Responsive teaching help students prepare themselves for managing their education by emphasizing both social and academic responsibility for their development. Furthermore, it emphasizes the promotion of racial-ethnic- linguistic equality and the appreciation of diversity within the process (Boyer, 1993).

Technology Use

Several educators argue that technology can enhance and supplement traditional classroom instruction as well as offer new ways to deliver instruction (NEA, 1998; Office of Technology Assessment, 1988, Olsen, 1990; Polin 1991;) . Some of the specific beneficial roles of technology that they discuss include; (a) fostering student's problem solving and higher level thinking and becoming an effective management tool for teachers and principals.

There is growing evidence that suggest that technology can significantly improve the education of students at risk of failure. Braun (1990), for example , examined several projects across the country that found that technology-enriched schools had a beneficial effect on student learning. He found several examples of technology that improved at-risk students's (a) attendance, (b) achievement, and (c) behavior. Descriptions of other major technology projects such as Wiburg (1991) all involve student at risk and all support Braun's findings. Furthermore, there have been several other studies that have found that technology has a positive impact on student at risk of failure.

There is also recent research that has examined the specific ways technology impacts students at risk. Hornbeck (1991), for example, list several generic characteristics of technology that helps student at risk; (a) motivational, (b) nonjudgmental, (c) individualizes learning, (d) allow for more autonomy, (e) gives prompt feedback and (f) allows for mastery of content at one's owns pace.

Computer-enriched instruction has the potential for deepening classroom instruction, making it more meaningful, and assisting the learning of higher order thinking skills (Niemiec, & Walberg, 1992). When technology is used this way as an instructional tool it can eliminate the pedagogy of poverty in urban classroom and empower all students with the thinking skills that will help them help themselves. Technology-enriched environments, however, are a new and very different instructional approach from what teachers have been exposed to in there other teachers education programs. Teachers, for the most part, have been trained with direct instructional, models, while technology-enriched instruction requires a student has some knowledge about technology that needs to be provided on a ongoing basis the school or district.

The three instructional approaches that are described in this article all have been found to be effective for teaching students at risk of failure and there are several benefits of incorporating these approaches in urban schools. The implementation of cognitively guided instruction has several positive components that can improve the education of students at risk. In reciprocal teaching for example, the text may either be read by the student or the teachers may read the text aloud to students. This technique can be very useful when teaching low-achieving student or limited-English proficient students who may experience a great deal of difficulty with the language.

Conclusion

Given the magnitude of the social problems facing many students in poverty, improving the quality of classroom instruction may appear to be only a small step towards correcting the serious problems facing these students. Exemplary classroom instruction, however, can increase students' self-esteem, academic achievement, and reduce their alienation and boredom. Furthermore, schools can become "islands of tranquility" in the lives of these students. They can provide students with quality adult-student relationships and supportive environments that minimize students' fears and promote a sense of belonging (Presidential Tasks

Force on Psychology in Education, 1993). Urban schools have the opportunity to provide these kinds of environment for all their students. Rather than reinforcing the negative experiences of failure, schools have the opportunity to help develop student's tolerance, sense of belonging, self-directness, teacher's work, cooperative learning, commitment, attitudes toward learning, participation, and engagement. The three instructional approaches described in the present article all Emphasize the sift form teacher-centered to students centered instruction , and they all focus on students' prior knowledge and cognitive learning. If teachers in urban schools begin to incorporate these instructional approaches then we can move from a "pedagogy of poverty" to a pedagogy of enrichment" (Brookhart & Rusnak, 1993). Consequently, improving the quality of instruction in urban schools may then first step toward reversing the cycle of educational failure.

References

Allington, R.L., & McGill-Franzen, A. (1989). School response to reading failure: Chapter 1 and special education students in grades 2, 4, & 8. *Elementary School Journal, 89*, 529-542.

Babad. E. (1990). Calling on students: How a teacher's behavior can acquire disparate meanings in students' minds. *Journal of Classroom Interaction, 25*, 1-4.

Boyd, W.L. (1991). What makes ghetto schools succeed or fail? Teachers College Record, 92, 331-362.

Boyer, J.B. (1993). Culturally-sensitive instruction: An essential component of education for diversity. *Catalyst for Change, 22*(3), 5-8.

Branch, R.C., Goodwin, Y., & Gualtieri, J. (1993). Making classroom instruction culturally pluralistic. The Educational Forum, 58, 59-70

Braun, L. (1990). *Vision: TEST final report: Recommendations for American educational decision makers*. Eugene, OR: International Society of Technology in Education.

Brookhart, S.M., & Rusnak, T.G. (1993). A pedagogy of enrichment, not poverty: Successful lessons of exemplary urban teachers. *Journal of Teacher Education, 44*(1), 17-26

Coley, J.D. & Hoffman, D.M. (1990). Overcoming learned helplessness in at risk readers. *Journal of Reading, 33*, 497-801.

Cuban, L. (1989). The "at risk" label and the problem of urban school reform. *Phi Delta Kappan*, 70, 780-784, 799-801.

Darder, A. (1993). How does the culture of the teacher shape the classroom experience of Latin students? The unexamined question in critical pedagogy. In S.W. Rothstein (Ed.) Handbook of schooling in urban America (pp. 195-221). Westport, CN: Greenwood.

Fletcher, T.V., & Cardona-Morlas, C. (1990). Implementing effective instructinal interventions for minority students. In A. Barona & E.E. Garica (Eds.), *Children at risk: Poverty, minority status, and others issues in educational equity* (pp. 151-170). Washington, DC: National Association of School Psychologists.

Foster, G.E. (1989). Cultivating the thinking skills of low achievers: A matter of equity. *Journal of Negro Education.* 58, 561-467.

Gagne, E. (1985). *The cognitive psychology of school learning.* Boston: Little Brown.

Gordon, E. W., & Yowell, C. (1994). Cultural dissonance as a risk factor in the development of students. In R.J. Rossi (Ed.), *Schools and students at risk* (pp. 51-69). New York: Teachers College Press.

Haberman, M. (1991). Pedagogy of poverty versus good teaching. *Phi Delta Kappan,* 73, 290-294.

Hornbeck, D.W. (1991). Technology and students at risk for school failure. In A.D. Sheekey (Ed.), *Educational policy and telecommunications technologies* (pp. 1-7). Washington, DC; U.S. Department of Education.

Irvin, J.L. (1992). Developmentally approprate instruction: The heart of the middle school. In J.L. Irvin (Ed.), *Transforming middle level education: Perspectives and possibilities* (pp.295-313). Boston: Allyn & Bacon.

Lehr, J.B. & Harris, H.W. (1998). *At risk, low-achieving students in the classroom.* Washington, DC: National Education Association.

Linn, M.C., & Songert, N.B. (1991). Cognitive and conceptual change in adolescence. American Journal of Education, 99, 379-417

Lucas, I., & Schecter, S.R. (1992). Literacy education and diversity: Toward equity in the teaching of reading and writing. *The Urban Review,* 24, 85-103

Means, B., & Knapp, M.S. (1991). Cognitive approaches to teaching advanced skills to educationally disadvantaged students. *Phi Delta Kappan,* 73, 282-289.

National Education Association. (1989). *The report of the NEA Special Committee on Educational Technology.* Washington, DC: National Education Association.

Niemiec, R.P., & Walberg, H.J. (1992). The effects of computers on learning. *International Journal of Educational Research,* 17, 99-108.

Olsen, J.B. (1990). Learning improvements results from integrated learning systems for underachieving minority students. In J.G. Bain & J.L. Herman (Eds.), *Making schools work for under-achieving minority students: Next steps for research policy, and practice* (pp. 241-255) Westport, CN: Greenwood Press.

Padron, Y.N., Knight, S.L., & Waxman, H.C. (1986). Analyzing bilingual and monolingual, students' perceptions of their reading strategies The Reading Teacher, 39, 430-433.

Polin, L. (1991). School restructuring and technology. *The Computing Teacher*, 18(6), 6-7.

Presidential Task Force on Psychology in Education. (1993). *Learner-centered psychological principles: Guidelines for school redesign and reform*. Washington, DC: American Psychological Association.

Pressley, M., & Ghatala, E.S. (1990). Self-regulated learning; Monitoring learning from text. *Educational Psychologist*, 25-19-33.

Sheingold, K. (1990). Restructuring for learning with technology: The potential for synergy. In K. Sheingold & M.S. Tucker (Eds.), *Restructuring for learning with technology* (pp. 9-27). New York: Center for Technology in Education, Bank Street College of Education.

Shields, P.M. (1991). School and community influences on effective academic instruction. In M.S. Knapp & P.M. Shields (Eds.), *Better schooling for the children of poverty: Alternatives to conventional wisdom* (pp. 313-328). Berkeley, CA; McCutchan.

Shuell, T.J. (1993). Toward and integrated theory of teaching and learning. Educational Psychologist, 28, 291-311.

Smey-Richman, B. (1993). *Teacher expectations and low-achieving students*. Philadelphia: Research for Better Schools.

Stein, M.K., Keinhardt, G., & Bickel, W. (1989) Instructional issues for teaching students at risk. In R.E. Slavin, N.L. Karweit, & N.A. Madden (Eds.), *Effective programs for students at risk* (pp. 145-194). Boston: Allyn & Bacon.

Stephen, V.P., Varble, M.E., & Taitt, H. (1993). Instructional strategies for minority youth. *The Clearing House*, 67, 116-120.

Waxman H.C. (1992). Reversing the cycle of educational failure for students in at-risk school environments. In H.C. Waxman, J. Walker de Felix, J. Anderson, & H.P. Baptiste (Eds.), *Students at risk in at risk schools: Improving environments for learning* (pp. 1-9). Newbury Park, CA: Corwin.

Wiburg, K.M. (1991a). Teaching teachers about technology, Computers in the Schools, 8(1/2/3), 115-129.

Winne, P.H. (1987). Why process-product research cannot explain process-product findings and a proposed remedy: The cognitive mediational paradigm. Teaching. Teaching and Teacher Education, 3, 333-356.

Chapter 12

Using the Whole-Language Approach with Minority Students

Students: Rhyme and Reason

Gwendolyn Duhon Boudreaux Ph.D.
McNeese State University

Katrina Boden-Webb, M.Ed.
Grambling State University

Jimmy McJamerson, M.A +68
Grambling State University

This chapter provides a definition and context for the concept of whole-language instruction. The whole-language approach to teaching is discussed and documentation is provided as to how students are positively impacted when reading stories about people from similar ethnic backgrounds and participating in activities that afford them opportunities to reflect and share their individual experiences. Sample lessons and literature using this approach will also be included.

There are various definitions or understandings about the concept a whole-language instruction. It has at times been referred to as a program, a process, or a theory (Clark, 1994). Some studies conclude that no facile definition existed, that whole-language balanced skills and creativity, and that teachers' understanding evolved as they continued to adapt their classrooms to their students' needs (Gross & Shefelbine,, 1991). Most succinctly, it is a set of beliefs about language, learning, and literary. Its' basic tenants are that

1. all learning is social:
2. language is learned through use; and
3. purpose and intention drive learning (Clark, 1994).

Whole language programs build upon a philosophy emphasizing the value of reader's knowledge of language and experiences and active involvement in constructing meaning from print (Goodman, 1986). Combined language experiences that integrate reading and writing, individualized reading, literature units, and child authored materials are educational practices that typify a language-centered reading approach (Zarillo, 1987).

Many traditional basal readers contain stories that tend to be far removed from the experiences of the readers and have little connection to real-life experiences. This is a major concern for minority students, who tend to find few commonalities with the characters and culture that is transmitted not only in the basals, but also in many urban public schools in the country. Children from minority and low-income families enter school with different pattern of communication and participation than those expected and reinforced by the school, which reflect the practices and competencies of the majority society and are constituted to protect and reproduce those practices. Students who arrived by the culture of the classroom are placed at disadvantages from the start (Davis, 1996).

By using a myriad of approaches that include using the readers' experiences as a context for understanding and responding to literature, whole language provides opportunities for success for minority students.

> "who are struggling in a system which demands independence in literacy for school success—yet which often fails to provide equal opportunities for that success" (Hollingsworth, Minarik, & Teel, 1990).

Whole-language allows students to take a more active role in the learning process by having them relate to the stories, their classmates, and even the teacher in new and innovative ways. Cooperative activities and student-authored materials create opportunities for students and teachers to respond to each other from positions of strengths, rather than engaging in the traditional process "of education in which those who transmit specific knowledge to those who don't know" (Gross & Shefelbine, 19911). Though the whole-language activities and student-generated materials, many minority students find their voices and an outlet for their untapped creativity. The students are engaged in activities that ate meaningful, directly related to the stories, and can enhance their self-esteem and ethnic pride. They can see themselves in the literature, and can find ways to show their talents through the literature-related activities.

The following is an example how literature (poetry) can be used in whole-language instruction to teach concepts in language arts, mathematics, social studies, science, and music. The following poem was chosen because of the strong connection between pride, knowledge of history, and success. Furthermore, the poem emphasizes all domains of education; cognitive affect, and psychomotor, while enhancing the self-esteem of both male and female students. This poem and subsequent activities are geared for 8th grade students.

I Am "Bad", And You Can't Stop Me

I shall, I will excel because I am bad, and you cannot stop me. I read everything because knowledge is power. In math, the Pythagorean theorem is as easy as 1,2,3. I can recite the poetry of Nikki Giovanni with ease, and I can play Beethoven's 5th Symphony with the fortitude of my being. You see, I am bad, and you can't stop me.

I can run with the best runners, keeping stride with Flo Jo and Carl Lewis. I can soar with the eagles like Michael Jordan when he puts on his show, for I am bad and you cannot stop me.

I can achieve, and will achieve. My inspiration comes from the Nubian Queen-Tiye; Bilalthe Islamic crier; Kunta Kinte- who rejected slavery; Phyllis Wheatley- the First African-American poetess; Joe Louis- the "Brown Bomber"; Barbara Jordan- the superb warrior/lawyer; Marva Collin- the ultimate teacher; Sammy Davis, Jr.- the master showman; Dr. M.L. King- the supreme leader; and Jimmy Jackson- the master politician. For I am bad, and you cannot stop me.

Like Prince Hall- the father of Black Masonic life, like John Johnson of Ebony and Jet, I can achieve and I will achieve. Like Dr. Daniel Hale Williams, who performed the first successful open heart surgery or Dr. Benjamin Carson, a neurosurgeon, I can excel in medicine, too. For I am bad and you cannot make me.

No drug pusher, nor pimp can stop; no racism, nor bigotry, nor injustice; for I am bad and you cannot stop me.

Like "Ice-T", I use my mind for a lethal weapon and like B. P. D. (Boogie Down Productions), I shall never forget my history, for I am bad and you cannot stop me.

Like Mohammad Ali, who declared, "I am the greatest", I now declared, I am bad, and you cannot stop me!

Jimmy McJamerson
Copyright, 1990

LANGUAGE ARTS

Objective: To teach students to distinguish and understand denotative and connotative meanings of words.

Materials Needed: Dictionary

Using the terms "I Am Bad" and "...as "deep" as Malcolm X." the teacher will discuss the meaning of the connotation (an implied meaning; a given meaning) and the denotation (dictionary meaning) of a word. The teacher will ask students to think of different meanings of the word "Bad". The teacher will write these meanings on the board. After discussion, the teacher should place words on the board that have both connotative and denotative meanings, e.g. dense, rat, blue, cool, fly, sharp, etc. Then, the class can be divided into pairs. Each pair is given a word to pantomimes the connotative meaning of a word while the other student pantomimes the denotative meaning of the word. Using both pantomimes, the students should be able to guess which word the pair is pantomiming.

MATH

Objective: To teach students to use the Pythagorean Theorem, a2 +b2= c2.

Materials: Counters to use as manipulatives, overhead projector

The teacher should explain that leg 2 +leg 2 = hypotenuse 2. Using an overhead projector the teacher after giving values for the variables "a", "b", and "c", can demonstrate the addition of the values and its sum. Furthermore, students can either work individually, in pairs, or as a cooperative group to demonstrate this concept. With the students sitting in pairs, give the class three numbers to serve as values for the letters "a", "b", and "c". Make sure that the numbers are small enough so that the students will have enough counters to square all the numbers. Have students to work along with you in their pair as you use your manipulatives on the overhead to demonstrate squaring each number and adding both "a" and "b". Afterwards, give each group three numbers to serve as values for the letter "a", "bn", and "c". After students have manipulated the counters to determine as answer, not necessary the right answer but an answer that pleases each group, have each pair to solve the problem using the overhead projector. Each pair will use their manipulative at their desks to model the group that is presenting. After presentations, students should work additional problems using the Pythagorean Theorem on paper. Students may use counters, if needed.

Extension: This poem can be use to introduce a unit on triangles. The lessons can include the parts of triangles (lines, angles, legs, and hypotenuses), the types of triangles, types of angles, and the measurements of a triangle, as well as its angles and sides.

SOCIAL STUDIES

Objective: To compare and contrast the American Executive branch of government to leader of an African tribal unit.

Materials: Weights of the same volume, balance beam

After discussion and lecture of the duties and functions of the two leaders, the teacher should demonstrate that although the types of governments are different, the duties and responsibilities are the same, they are equal. One weight should be place on the balance beam for overall duties and/or responsibilities for each of the leaders ,e.g. one weight each for governing the welfare of its people, one weight for each leader for solving the problems of its people, and so forth.

Extension: Either of the great achievers from this poem and their achievements can be discussed as social studies lessons. Tiye and Kunta Kinte can be great anticipatory sets for a unit on Africa. Dr. Martin Luther king, Jr. is a great person to begin a discussion on the Civil Rights Movement or a study of the South during different periods of time. Furthermore, a unit can be developed on the three branches of government; the people that are involved in each branch, the reason for each branch, each branch's role and responsibilities, and how people become qualified to serve on either branch.

SCIENCE

Objective: After discussion and class participation, the learner will be able to describe the heart and the position of the ventricles, atriums, and aorta and their functions.

Materials: Model or picture of the heart, stethoscope (can be borrowed from the school nurse) clay, straws, and markers.

As an anticipatory set, the student can be allowed to listen to their heartbeat through the stethoscope. After lecture and discussion, the students will be given a piece of clay, large Clay to demonstrate the location of the ventricles, atriums, and the aorta. The students should color the straw, having the strews representing the ventricles one color, the straws representing the atrium another color, and the aorta being one distinct color. Each model of the heart can be saved for use in other lessons relating to the heart.

Extension: Dr. Daniel Hale Williams opens the door for a unit on he circulatory system and/or organs of the body. Moreover, there may be detailed lessons about the heart, the functions of veins and arteries, and maintaining a healthy body.

CREATIVE ARTS – MUSIC

Objective: To introduce students to a variety of songs performed by Sammy Davis, Jr.

Materials: 3-4 songs that were performed by Sammy Davis, Jr.

The teacher can present information about the legendary Sammy Davis, Jr. Afterward, students listen to a variety of his music and can discuss he types of songs that he performed.

In summary, whole-Language represents a shift form the traditional form of reading and language arts instruction that has dominated in American public schools. This approach affords minority students opportunities to interact with literature in a way that allows them to demonstrate their linguistic talent as well as become active, necessary participants in the teaching and learning process.

References

Clark, K. (1994). *Whole language and language-minority students: A natural fit.* (ERIC Document Reproduction Service No. ED 379 946).

Davis, A. (1996). Successful urban classrooms as communities of practice; Writing and identity. (ERIC Document Service No. ED 414 584).

Goodman, K. (1996). *What's whole in whole language?* Portsmouth, NH: Heinemann.

Gross, P., & Shefelbin, J. (1991). Whole language teacher education in multicultural contexts: Living our own models of learning. (ERIC Document Reproduction Service No. ED 359 489).

Hollingsworth, S., Minarik, L., & Teel, K. (1991). Listening for Aaron: A teacher's story about modifying a literature-based approach to literacy to accommodate a young male's voice. East Lansing. MI: National Center for Research on Teacher Learning. (ERIC Document Reproduction Service No. ED 346 082).

Zarillo, J. (1987, August). Literature-centered reading and language minority. Paper presented for the Institute on Literacy and Learning Language Minority Project, University of California.

CHAPTER 13

LIERACY IN THE EARLY YEARS

Phyllis C. Cuevas Ph.D.
McNeese State University

What is literacy?

Literacy begins in the home as parents introduce children to reading and writing by modeling these activities and by providing the materials of reading and writing. They also endow their children with an attitude toward reading and writing. This introduction to literacy lays the foundation for subjects studied in school. Literacy can be defined as reading and writing. Some educators broaden that definition to include all the communication skills: reading, writing, speaking, viewing, and listening (Cooper, 1997). Other educators would also include the use of technology as a tool for communicating (Thornburg, 1992).

Emergent literacy is a term that was first used by Marie Clay to explain how "children acquire knowledge about language, reading, and writing" before entering school (Clay, 1966). Children explore their environment and in do8ing so make observations about reading and writing. They see the print filing their world and notice the various ways writing is used. Formal instruction in reading and writing typically begins in kindergarten.

What Knowledge of literacy do young children bring to school?

Young children enter school with a wealth of knowledge about language and how it is used. By the time children are four years old, most have a speaking-listening vocabulary of 4,000 words (Petty, 1994). These words are the basis for learning to read. Children can typically recognize their own name and the names of favorite restaurants such as "McDonalds or Wendy". They can recognize the name of their favorite candy or cereal and many can read traffic signals. Four-year olds are beginning to recognize letters of the alphabet in the world around them. Children whose parents read to them know that a story has a beginning and an end. They know that the words tell the story even if they are not sure what a word is.

They have begun to experiment with writing and sometimes make a scribble that looks like a letter of the alphabet. Young children bring much knowledge about literacy to the school setting.

Literacy Suggestions for Preschool children

The following suggestions are offered for developing the emerging literacy skills of the preschool child:

1. Read to the child often.
   A. Begin with books with simple story lines, many pictures, and few words. When the child tires of the book, put it away until later. Reading with a child should be pleasurable.

   B. Read favorite books over and over again. Let the child help with the reading of the story by supplying last worlds of sentence.
   C. Read with expression. Act out the story and have fun.
   D. Make reading to the child a part of the daily routing.
   E. Children should see adults reading in their daily life. Adults reading newspapers, recipes, or directions help children see the importance of reading.
2. Allow children to write.

   A. Children begin with scribbling. Provide blank paper and a variety of writing instruments.
   B. Painting helps children to develop writing skills.
   C. Playing with clay develops the small muscles needed for writing.
   D. Children begin with tearing of paper and then progress to cutting with scissors as their muscles develop. Cutting with scissors help to develop the small muscles in the hand needed for writing.
   E. Drawing pictures is one way to communicate. Show children how to write by drawing a picture.
3. Talk with the child.

A. Talk about actions and events. "Today we are going to the bank. I need to cash a check so that we can buy you some new shoes."
B. Listen to children when they are talking because this teaches that what the child has to say is important.
C. Use the correct name for objects in the child's world. Instead of saying "Hand me that thing on the table," say, Hand me the remote control for the television.". Teach children the names of trees and flowers and other objects found in the world.
D. Teach children nursery rhymes and songs. The language of rhymes helps children learn to read and teach them about beginning and ending sounds.

Use every opportunity to expose children to reading and writing. For example, young children enjoy helping adults with cooking simple recipes. They can pour liquids or other ingredients into a bowl and stir. They can listen as the adult reads off the list of ingredients and careful measures each. This help the young child see the importance of reading.

The Value of Literature

A child is never too young to hear stories read aloud (Trelease, 1989). Some parents even read or play music for the child in the womb believing that this gives the child an early start on learning. Parents start by reading simple books with many pictures. Book with short sentences and much action hold the attention of small children. The child can interact with the book by asking questions and talking about the story. Listening to books and watching as the parent reads teaches the child basic concepts about print including:

1. Print is written left to right and top to bottom.
2. A book has a front and a back.
3. Words on a page can tell a story.
4. Writing consists of works, sentences, and paragraphs.
5. A word is made of letters of the alphabet.

Literacy in the Early Childhood Grades

Most children begin their formal schooling in kindergarten, although many attend preschool or child care before age five. The literacy instruction or exposure that began at home continues in the setting of the school. The emphasis in the early years is upon learning through play. As children interact with their environments, they use reading and writing in he school setting. Instruction is informal and arises out of the daily activities of the child.

Reading in the Early Grades

The early childhood classroom is a place where children are immersed in language, reading, and writing to facilitate literacy. Language and take dominate the day's activities. Children talk to their classmates and to their teacher and anyone else that happens to come into the classroom. Children become proficient speakers by using language daily in a variety of ways.

Reading activities play a key role in the early childhood classroom. Children hear quality literature read with expression and within interest and enthusiasm. Children want t read when adults model a love of reading. Books are placed thought the room. A reading listening center is a place where children can find a comfortable place to read books. The books reflect a variety of topics and interests. Many teachers like to change the selection of books periodically.

Writing in the Early Grades

In the early grades children have many opportunities to practice writing skills. Writing centers have a variety of kinds and colors of paper to use for writing and a variety of writing instruments. Small scrapes of paper are often the perfect choice for a sign or name to label an art project or block structure. Writing is encouraged as a way of expressing one's thoughts. Teachers may ask children with a problem to write it down in a "Problems Notebook". Activities such as this show that writing is useful and valued.

Young children to through predictable stages in learning to write. First, they scribble. Next, the scribbling begins to resemble print. Children begin to approximate letter of the alphabet and numbers. During this stage most children first learn to read and write their name. This is a practical skill for it allows the teacher to label a special space for each child's belongings. Having each child label his or her own drawings, writings, and are project, rather than have the teacher write the name of each child is useful. Children who have difficulty writing their name. Especially of the name is long or has many difficult letters such as "s", will often scribble their name or writing their first initial. Even these forms are recognizable by the child and the teacher.

Reading, writing, and language are a part of every activity and used throughout the day. As children study about animals in science, they draw pictures or write about what they learned. They discuss their new knowledge with another classmate or with the teacher. They read many books about animals. In physical education classes, children keep a record of the skills they have learned, such a how many times they can jump rope without missing or how far they can jump. This helps children to see the reading and writing is part of everyday life and not just something we do in school.

SUMMARY

Research consistently reminds us that the early years from birth to age eight are crucial for learning (Cole, 1993). The four-year-old can easily learn a foreign language that seems impossible for the twenty-year old. During these early years, parents and educators have a grave responsibility for providing a wealth of opportunities in reading, writing and language for each young child. These activities are the foundation of literary.

Reference

Clay, M.M. (1966). Emergent reading behavior. Doctoral dissertation, University of Aukland, New Zealand

Cole, Michael and Cole, Sheila R. (1993). The development of children. New York: Scientific American Books, p. 335.

Cooper, J. David (1997) Literacy: Helping children construct meaning. Boston: Houghton Mifflin Company, p. 7.

Petty, Walter T., Petty Dorothy C., and Salzer, Richard T. (1994). Experiences in language. Boston: Allyn & Bacon, p. 197.

Thornburg, D. (1992). Edutrends. San Carlos, California: Starsong Publishers.

Trelease, Jim (1989). The new read-aloud handbook. New York: Penguin Press.

Chapter 14

At-Risk Students Who are They?

Tony J. Manson, Ph.D.
Austin Peay State University

This article is a history of the treatment and consideration given in American education to students who are now classified as "at-risk". The term is a relatively recent coinage, reflecting the newness of educators' recognition that a measurable portion of students, beyond those with evident physical or mental handicaps, have special educational needs. Comprehending what educators mean by the term "at-risk." which has become more an acknowledgement of economic disadvantage and less a categorization of biological abnormalities, is essential to understanding the ways in which such children have been treated throughout the development of the educational system in the United States.

Concepts and Semantics

Historically, the concept of compulsory education for all as an individual right and a societal necessity developed while the United States grew and matured as not an industrialized nation. The changing way in which educators have looked on the problems presented by "at-risk" children represents a striking model for their refinement in thinking about education as a whole. From early Colonial times, when schooling was considered to be primarily the responsibility of the family, to the modern age of widespread societal involvement in educational systems that attempt to include the entire young population, the varying needs of the individual child continue to pose a complicated challenge to each successive generation.

Educators began to talk about "at-risk" students during the 1970s but still have not agreed on a precise definition of the term. While it may include students with physical or emotional handicaps, learning disabilities, or other special education needs, "at-risk" has come to focus primarily on children of poverty, those from poorer single-parent homes, and those without homes at all. Stephen B. McCarney

(1991) writes: "

"At-Risk" means different things to different people. To the teacher, "At-Risk" may mean the student is "At-Risk" for failure which will result in retention at the end of the year. To the social worker, "At-Risk" may mean that an abused child is "At-Risk for becoming an abusive parent. To the social or economic analyst, an "At-Risk child is one who is born out of wedlock, grows up in poverty and is likely to repeat the cycle (p.3)

Barbara Z. Presseisen (1991) writes, "At-Risk" appears to be the latest semantic label of American education attached to several groups of students who have experienced difficulty or, in fact, failure in their careers as learners (p.5). She lists some of the other labels that "at-risk" has come to encompass: "culturally deprived, low income, dropout, alienated, marginal, disenfranchised, impoverished, underprivileged, disadvantaged, learning disabled, low performing ,low achieving, remedial, urban ghetto, language-impaired" (p.5). The term most often links children whose learning difficulties arise form the complications of poor economic backgrounds.

A Symptom Dyslexia

Dyslexia is among the most common learning disabilities exhibited by at-risk children; It is a disability that has only recently been widely examined and analyzed. While a diagnosis of dyslexia does not automatically place a child at risk, this barrier to learning is often present in those children facing other obstacles, adding to their difficulties in the classroom. Presseisen (1991) contends, "As much as 15 percent of the entire population may exhibit symptoms of various handicapping conditions akin to dyslexia" (p.9). The "at-risk category also includes those who cannot speak or read English well, since this places students at a distinct disadvantage in the classroom, where most progress is tied to reading, listening, and speaking proficiency.

The State of Education

Lawrence A. Cremin (1976) notes that public education arose out of "the interest of equalizing opportunity and encouraging individual development and at the same time achieving a certain measure of socialization for public ends" (p. 124). As cities and factories grew, American society realized the unusefulness of being able to communicate with thousands of fellow citizens able to read street signs, calculate transactions, and record sales order. Perhaps even more important. Society began to see the value of schools providing a sense of community, which was no longer possible to achieve in any other way within the swelling urban environment. The rise of cities and the new middle class made at least minimal education for the poor a social imperative: despite their best efforts, members of the upper class were unable to completely avoid contact with the lower classes in the modern world.

The United States has grown to the point that the handicapped, the very slow, the very young, the emotionally disturbed, the gifted have all received attention to form the concept of inclusion. Also, the concept that education should be available and mandatory for all children has let to the belief that tax-supported schools are necessary to a democratic society, an idea that was not universally accepted at first. In the early part of this century, at-risk students were mot often defined be their economic disadvantages, this disparity resulted in an even greater educational imbalance in high-density urban center, a situation not foreseen by scholars and educators who championed universal education as a democratic ideal.

Atkinson and Malesk (1962) write, "Several million American children are handicapped in ways that demand specialized education facilities. A report made to the Fourth White House Conference in the 1940's reported tat approximately 30 percent of all children in American schools could be grouped into what is writers termed at the time the "delicate child" class. In the 1990s that figure has at least tripled. As educators started to address the particular education needs of "delicate" children openly, they developed separate classes and in many cases separate schools within the same district to deal with these children. Separating out students, however, proved to be less-than-popular concept, and the arguments gave way to "mainstreaming" special needs student back into regular classrooms as much as possible. Today these facilities are no different than any other. Facility on a high school campus. In many cases they are no more than a room or a section of the school that is usually forbidden for "regular student's to be near. In fact many school district have what is usually forbidden for 'regular students' to be near. In fact many **school** districts have what is known as 'Alternative Schools'. These schools are designed specially for student at-risk of dropping out of school because of most anything (addictions, attendance, attitude, behavior, etc...).

Categories

The "at-risk" diagnosis is a recent attempt by educators to gather together all those categories of children with problems that prevent them from progressing unaided within a regular classroom. Theses include students with attention deficit disorder (ADD), as well as those deemed educable mentally impaired (EMI), educable mentally retarded (EMR), emotionally impaired (EI), and even those informally diagnosed as "troublemakers". Valerie Polakow (1993) quotes a Phi Delta Kappa study in which "The authors begin with the assumption "that children are at risk if they are likely to fail-either in school or in life"" (p. 153).

One of the older labels, learning disabled (LD), continues to provide subtly different meaning in the educational debate. Gerald Coles (1987) explains:
The category was introduced in the U.S. schools in the 1960s as one of the means of explaining a handicapping condition which many professional and middle-class parents considered unadessed by existing educational classifications... [They] thought that special-education classifications such as "mentally retarded' or emotionally disturbed" and prevailing social-science categories for explaining academic failure such as "culturally deprived" seemed more appropriate for children from minority and poor communities, not children from the middle class (p. xiii).

Coles observed that in recent years educators have3 applied the LD diagnosis much more broadly, prompting middle-class parents to seek other labels in order to maintain distinctions between students who enjoy economic advantage and children of poverty. "At-risk" has become one of the most useful of these labels.

Otherness

Increasingly, however, this kind of political abuse of educational diagnoses has come under fire. Polakow (1993) contends, "We call [Students] 'at risk' less out of outrage and compassion than because their condition threatens our security and comfort, our children, our schools, our neighborhoods, our property values. Their otherness places us 'at-risk' " (p.43). Coles (1987) summarizes a number of studies showing that minority children tend to be represented in "at-risk" grouping in disproportionately high numbers in many parts of the country, suggesting that such categories " allowed discrimination to continue but in a less blatant form" (p. 206).

As America began to accept the need for universal free education, educators only belatedly came to see that this would require systems flexible enough to accommodate individual differences. They grouped these differences into diagnosable categories, naming and renaming categories for semantic clarity and political fashion. "At-risk" is the most recent category name to specify a group of students always present in the population, the "deserving poor," children who have never fit easily into any mainstream conception of American education.

References

Atkinson, C., and Maleska, E. T. (1962). The Story of Education. Philadelphia: Chilton.

Coles, G. (1987). The Learning Mystique: A Critical Like at "Learning Disabilities" New York: Pantheon.

Cremin, L.A. (1976). Traditions of American Education. New York; Basic.

McCarney, S.B. (1991). The At-Risk Student in Our Schools: A Model intervention Program for the At-Risk Student's Most Common Learning and Behavioral Problems. Columbia, MO: Hawthorne Educational Services.

Polakow, V. (1993). Lives on the Edge: Defining a Population. In K.M. Kershner. J.A. Connolly (eds.), At-Risk Students and School Restructuring (pp. 5-11). Philadelphia: Research for Better Schools.

Chapter 15

From Under prepared To Academic Success:

A Case for Student-Athlete Support Programs and Their Priorities

Craig Curry, M..A
Albany State University

"We seem to be the only country on earth whose children fall farther behind the longer they stay in school" according to the Thomas B. Fordham Foundation "A Nation Still at Risk, An Education Manifesto". This is true of our advanced students and our so-called good schools, as well as those in the middle. Remediation is rampant in college, with some 30% of entering freshman (including more than half at the sprawling California State University System) in need of remedial courses in reading, writing and mathematics. The report goes on to say that the U.S. Silicon Valley entrepreneurs press for higher immigration levels so they can recruit the qualified personnel they need.

These scary statistics coupled with the "disincentive" to appear intelligent in the urban communities, leave many African Americans, especially males walking a tight rope between the school and the streets (Viadero, D. Two Different Worlds, Part I, Education Week, July 1997).

To some degree, all children who are singled out as gifted have a tough time moving between their academic worlds and the everyday culture of teenage life. For black kids from low income families, those challenges can be especially trying. Besides all the usual hardships, their peers might accuse them of "acting white" because they are succeeding in a world whose rhythms and norms reflect white society. So some hide their intelligence.

In the State of Georgia where the black/white comparison could use drastic reforms when it comes to academic preparation and academic success at the college level, shows just how wide the academic gap is.

Future student-athletes, parents and teachers along with all African Americans should be aware of the academic process in our public schools. The intense recruitment of black student-athletes to major academic institutions solely on their athletic ability is cause for alarm. A UCLA study found that black families are four times more likely than white families to view their children's involvement in athletics as something that may lead to a professional sports career (Frank, G. (1991) Major Violation).

The total population of K-12 enrollment for the school year 1996-97 was 1.3 million (57% white and 37% black) in the state of Georgia. For the school year 1997-98 the total number of school children retained were 57,075, 41% white 53% blacks. The average retention increase was 4% white, 6% black. Out of 67,407 gifted students, 86% was white and 11% were black. Out of 22,412 in special education (retarded), 32% were white and 65% were black. Of the 11,016 that was learning disorder, 69% white and 27% black. And of the 29,249 students in the college prep program, 67% were white and 28% were black.

Why such a disparity in success? Why such a high percentage of African Americans in Special Education and such a low number in Learning Disabilities classes? Why such low numbers of African Americans graduating in the College Prep area? These questions are beyond the scope of this paper and must be discussed in another article. However, the trend is not pretty. There are a number of factors, but one crucial point that Rosenthal and Jacobson concluded was that a person's place in society is largely a matter of how he or she is treated by others, and they said a student's intellectual development is largely a response to what teachers <u>expect</u> and how those expectations are communicated (Rosenthal, R. & Jacobson, L. PYGMALION In the Classroom, 1968).

I submit to you that racism whether conscience or unconscience, plays a big role. Here is an example: "For 12 years, civil rights enforcers said nothing about the way Georgia Schools assigned students to classes. But the past year, at least five Georgia districts, including Early and Evans Counties, have forced the loss of federal funds for diverting students into advanced, average and slow classrooms in a way that federal investigators found had no legitimate educational purpose. In case after case, Black children who outscored White classmates on standardized test were steered into the low track anyway, investigators found. Meanwhile, whites were elevated into the top classes regardless of low scores." (The Atlanta Journal, The Atlanta Constitution Sunday, Dec. 11, 1994, pp. G1, G4. G5. "Who's Smart Who's Not side tracked Into Special Education".

I wonder how many other states have similar policies and practices. Reforms for long term inclusion in a society that has a history of racism must begin in the public elementary schools so the gap doesn't continue to widen eliminating some from college. The talent of athletics can't always be the determining factor on whether someone goes to college, because academic standards are changing there too. Making assignments easy for student-athletes must not be tolerated. What happens to the non-athlete who gets the "steady dose of low level, boring, if not down right silly assignments and curricula" in some middle and high school? (Dougherty & Barth). Will those assignments prepare one for passing the state exam?

Now take those same students and put them in high profile universities on athletic scholarships and the need for academic support becomes obvious. Also, the exploitative factor seems inevitable. Student-athletes without proper support succumb to the "just stay eligible" factor of college life. Unless a professionally assembled support program is in place for the student-athlete.

Student-Athlete Support Programs are often criticized by faculty and non student-athletes. They are looked upon as special services for athletes that are not available to the general student population. Yet, other institutional staff claim that student-athlete support programs are a duplication of effort of what academic units currently provide. Which is true? The answer lies somewhere in between.

What distinguishes student-athletes from the rest of the student body is their commitment to their scholarship and NCAA rules and regulations. While at the same time progressing towards a meaningful diploma. This is why these services exist and must hire knowledgeable staff members, and have in place measurable progressive instruments for academic follow-up.

Beginning with the "recruited" student-athletes (in football and basketball for Division I schools) many are "special admissions" to the university, often with significant remedial needs (Gerdy, The Successful Athletic Program). "If the university admits under-prepared student-athletes for the purpose of generating money and exposure, it must also assume responsibility for developing a support system to allow those "special admits" an opportunity to succeed academically and socially". I agree with Mr. Gerdy when he says, "Faculty concern regarding special treatment is understandable, or long as colleges and universities continue to accept student-athletes who are less prepared academically than the general student body, and at the same time demand significant amounts of time and effort for peak athletic performance, special academic support programs cannot be termed a luxury; rather they are an institutional responsibility".

To fulfill institutional obligations, the student-athlete must travel out of town, usually missing one or more days out of class. A minimum of 12 credit hours must be maintained or they become immediately ineligible. So, if a course of study is bringing a grade point average down, unlike the regular student who can drop a class and fall below 12 hours, the student-athlete cannot. Finally, student-athletes practice a minimum of twenty hours per week (By-Law NCAA Manual) usually year round most even more when you add film time. Giving their peers at least that amount of time (3 ½ to 4 hours a day) to devote to academic matters (i.e. studying, professor office visits, career seminars, etc).

In developing a student-athlete program, the total person approach must be pursued. Not just maintaining an acceptable grade point average or keeping student-athletes eligible for competition but the social, psychological, and career needs must be met.

These study sessions or "study table" as they are called, must be organized with proctors and tutors available preferably at a location integrating with non-student athletes around so they are not feeling isolated with the same faces they practice with all week. This would also offer a sense of social development and allow the student body to see the student-athletes in a non athletic environment.

These sessions must require that work is done no matter how exhausted the student-athletes are and to ensure integrity, the student-athlete must sign in and out with work completed and signed by the tutor. Contact with professors should be made periodically with comments of the progress of the student-athlete. Most schools have to go as far as class checks as a part of the monitoring system to ensure attendance.

Life after athletics is an extremely important foundational benefit of any student-athlete services program.

The danger is enrolling student-athletes in courses that will keep them eligible for competition rather than allowing the freedom to choose and expand their intellectual curiosity. The results are a diminished opportunity to graduate or a transcript full of elective or irrelevant courses.

With the proper personnel running the program, it becomes more than just basic tutoring and skills development. It can include an array of activities such as, assessment and placement, curriculum design and delivery and evaluation (The Institute for Higher Education Policy, (Dec. 1998) College Remediation).

Assessment and placement would include instruments of assessing reading, writing and mathematics. But critical to the process must be a measurement to include learning style, study skills and career interest.

Curriculum design would enable the student-athlete to work both independently and in groups, to ensure different learning styles are addressed and a flexible delivery of the curriculum must be available. Learning outcomes are spelled out to evaluate student achievement.

Evaluation process measures the transition of college level courses from high school curriculum, assessment of the effectiveness of the support program, and are the student-athletes reaching their academic goals? These areas will prove the "quality" of an effective program.

The other key factor for the student-athlete support program is a knowledgeable staff of tutors, counselors, and graduate assistants, not just there for the glamour of the high profile contact, but trained for one-on-one sessions focused on academic development.

As Claude Steele's research and documentation has indicated, a majority of African Americans succeed in the most challenging college classes like chemistry, calculus and engineering when proper support and encouragement is given.

There is an obvious connection between our public school education and academic success in college. "The academic problems facing intercollegiate athletics are those plaguing the American educational system as a whole. Literacy and basic skills for the poor and minorities, appropriate educational goals for an evolving economy, sensible and fair testing procedures, the formulation of adequate exit standards, the redressing of funding inequities, and the retention of students themselves are broad issues with which all educators must grapple. As long as such problems exist at the public school level, NCAA institutions will continue to face academic athletic dilemmas". (Funk, F. {1991} Major Violation)

REFERENCES

Booker, C. (1998) The State of Black Male America
http: www.tomco.net/~afimale/stbm98.htm

Brock, R. Deconstructing Black Academic Underachievement. http:www.mcnair.barkelye.edu/UGA/OSL/McNair/93 Barkeley McNair

Jo.../RochelleBrock.htm

Comer, J. (1997) Waiting For a Miracle, Why schools can't solve our problems - and how we can.

Cotton, K. And Wikeland, K. School Improvement Research Series (SIRS) Expectations and Student Outcomes. http.www.nwrel.org/scpd/sirs/41cu7.html

Dougherty, E. and Barth, P. (April 1997) Education Week on the Web, How to Close the Achievement Gap www.edduweek.com/ew/vol-16/27dough.h16

Funk, G. (1991) Major Violation: The Unbalanced Priorities in Athletics and Academics

Gerdy, J. (1997) The successful athletic program. Onyx Press

Hendrie, C. (Jan.1998) Education Week on the Web, Alienation From H.S. is worst among Black Males, Study Reveals. www.edweek.com/ew/vol-17/20esteem.h17

Porter, M. (1997) Kill Them Before They Grow, Misdiagnosis of African American Boys in American Classrooms.

Shropshire, K. (1996) In Black & White, Race and Sports in America

Thomas B. Fordham Foundation, A Nation Still at Risk An Education Manifesto (April 1998) www.edexcellence.net/library/manifes.html

Viadero, D. (July 1997) Two Different Worlds, Education Week on thee Web. www.edweek.com/ew/vol-16/40gift.h16

The Institute for Higher Education Policy. (Dec. 1998) College Remediation, What it is, What it cost, What's at stake. Strategies for Achieving Equity(Part3) www.enc.org/reform/journals/ENC24330/2430-3.htm

Georgia Dept. Of Education & Council on School Performance of Georgia State Univ. Georgia Statistics on Racial Gaps in Public Schools Education

Chapter 16
Educational Programs; Turning Victims into Survivors

Jerry Hardee, Ph.D.
Vice President Academic Affairs
Albany State University

Alice Duhon-Ross Ph.D.
Albany State University

Ethelyn Lumpkin, Graduate Student
Albany State University

School districts across America are building partnerships with Universities and the business sector to address the needs of children who are victims of poverty. According to the 1990 poverty statistics referenced for the Georgia Policy Council on Children and Families there are counties were 75 percent of the families live in poverty. Nationally the majority of at-risk youths are victims of poverty and the circumstances impeding in their learning can be viewed as at-risk. has become a major concern for many school systems. The traditional reform programs, attempt to solve the problems of students falling behind in their grades, failing classes and the prevention of teenage pregnancies are no longer considered exclusive concerns in resolving the many ills of student problems. For example, traditional programs designed to prevent illegal drug usage and teenage pregnancies often used scare tactics to achieve their expected preventive goals. The method utilized proved unsuccessful and drug use/teenage pregnancies continued within the student population.

Today however, many concerns, some unique to geographical areas, ethnic groups, economical status are plaguing students and school systems across the country. The concerns are forcing school faculty, staff and administrators to reconsider their traditional methods of assisting students and restructuring their educational curriculum to accommodate the at-risk population of students by offering appropriate classes, programs and training as needed to achieve a positive learning environment. One such program primarily new to many school systems includes components of life skills incorporated with drug education, sex education, as an effort to induce independent thinking, positive self-concept, and positive self-esteem amongst participants. Additionally, Bilingual education and multicultural education are of concern in school systems having a student population from many cultures. Programs are designed to stimulate mutual respect within the student population, for those who are different in regards to race, sex, physical abilities and beliefs. Such programs are needed to combat negativity displayed by students and to enhance tolerance levels through awareness.

Also, resulting from the many concerns, problems and societal dilemmas thought to cause interference in the educational process of students, outside agencies and individuals are being utilized to assist at-risk students. Such a collaborative effort requires strict enforcement of guidelines set by sponsors in order for programs to achieve success and remain within the school systems established rules. The following programs are currently operating in Southwest Georgia. These programs are making a tremendous difference in providing alternatives to enhance students learning regardless of their circumstances.

Mitchell County Children and youth, Inc., a collaborative program was started in 1990 as a resource to address problems with children and families in Mitchell County, Georgia. (Bostick, 1996) The agency set objectives and goals to be achieved by the year 2000 to include the following: Healthy Children, children ready for school, children succeeding in school, Mitchell County Children and Youth (MCCY) envisioned that "all Mitchell County children will become literate, healthy, productive citizens and all Mitchell county families will become stable and economically self-sufficient. The agency identified a target population of students in three local schools; Mitchell County Primary, Mitchell County Elementary and Pelham Elementary Schools who exhibit three established risk factors. Mitchell County Children and Youth's purpose for operating a case management program is listed as the following;

"(1) To identify students in grades K-5 who exhibit established risk factors;

(2) To assign referred student to an MCCY Case Manager;

(3) To make personal contact with caretakers of identified students, offering MCCY case management services;

(4) To obtain caretaker's written consent to participate in MCCY Case Management Program;

(5) To gather appropriate information on referred student from caretaker, school personnel and other agency representatives who may have worked with the student or family;

(6) To develop care plan for MCCY program participant with input from all available resources;

(7) To network program participants to all needed resources in Mitchell County;

(8) To provide extensive case management and follow-up for program participants for a maximum of three years; and

(9) To monitor program participants after three years of intensive case management until high school graduation" (Bostick, 1996).

The Mitchell County Children and Youth Mental Health Program is another division of Mitchell County Children and Youth. The purpose of the this program is to "to provide Mental Health services to at-risk children/adolescents and their families to enhance life satisfaction and to promote community and family functioning. The target population for this program is children and adolescents who may benefit from Mental Health Services.

The objectives of this program are:

"(1) To accept referrals made to Mental Health Services;

(2) To make personal contact with child and guardian to be informed of presenting problem;

(3) To obtain cartaker's written consent to participate in Mental Health services;

(4) To obtain information from school personnel and other agency representatives who may have worked with child and/or family;

(5) To identify a need for Mental Health services and provide a Diagnostic

Statistical Manual-IV diagnostic impression;

(6) To develop an Individualize Service Plan for child from all information gathered;

(7) To provide psychological assessment and refer child for a psychiatric evaluation within 45 days of the assessment;

(8) To present the child's case to be licensed clinical supervisor for recommendation of appropriate interventions;

(9) To provide individual, family, and group therapy as recommended to help client meet Individualized Service Plan goals;

(10) To review Individualized Service Plan on a quarterly basis and make appropriate changes as child progresses through therapy;

(11) To update all information on a yearly basis; and

(12) To monitor child's progress for three years or until age 18 (Bostick, 1996).

Mitchell County Children and Youth, Inc. operates a Youth Advisory Council (MCYAC) with a purpose of developing and implementing ways to improve the status of youth in Mitchell County. The Youth Advisory Council address the problems of teen pregnancy, drugs, gangs and drop out using preventive programs mentorship role modeling, community involvement and interaction.

The Mentoring program offered by Mitchell County Children and Youth, Inc. targets students in the Pelham, Georgia City Schools and Mitchell County school system who need mentors. The purpose of the mentoring program is "to encourage the community to exercise a responsibility and a need to support the educational system through a volunteer mentoring program for at-risk students. The objectives of the program is to improve the self-esteem and academic performance of students through tutoring in academic areas, positive role modeling one-on-one interaction and encouraging the students efforts towards improvement.

Mitchell County Children and Youth, Inc. also offer prevention programs. This is done in an effort to make the community more aware of the needs for prevention in matters that affect the youth. Preventive information is offered in the form of pamphlets, videos, books, models, and curriculum.

Youth Experiencing Success (YES) is an after school program provided by Mitchell County Children and Youth, Inc. The program aims to assist students academically and socially in the form of tutoring, counseling, recreation, social intervention and parental involvement. The program targets fourth and fifth grade students in the Mitchell County Elementary School are one year or more below grade level in reading and/or math. YES objectives are to improve test scores and grade point averages, prevent grade retention and achieve school attendance rates for participants, equivalent to the overall average school attendance rate of students.

Postponing Sexual Involvement in an educational series for young teens that is offered by Mitchell County Children and Youth, Inc. The purpose of the program is to assist young people with developing skills to resist pressure to become sexually involved outside the context of marriage. The program is offered to students in middle to high school grades in Mitchell County Schools. The objectives of the program are to help young people to understand the pressures of society influencing sexual behavior, understand their rights in relationships, avoid situations that might lead to sexual involvement prior to marriage; deal with pressure situations using assertive responses, postpones premarital sexual involvement.

2000 Friends is a mentoring program "sponsored by Dougherty County School System, Albany Dougherty 2000 Partnership, the Children and Youth Coordinating Council of Georgia, the Pew Partnership for Civic Change, the Renaissance Centre and the Southwest Georgia Regional Mental Health Mental Retardation and Substance Abuse Board, a continuation of flood crisis counseling services to children and youth" (Mentor Manual 2000 Friends). The program was designed as a direct result of the flood, 1994 and to help young people achieve academic success, increase self esteem, gain knowledge about jobs and job opportunities and to identify potential problems.

The program's goals are to assist students with dealing with their specific needs resulting from the flood, 1994, discover their strengths and skills, gain self respect, increase their knowledge of community resources, improve their goal setting and goal achieving abilities and recognize the connection between education and work. "Mentors will serve as true friends to their protégé. They are not meant to take the place of parents or teachers. On the contrary, their goals are to complement and enhance the efforts being made at home and at school to transform a child into a responsible and productive adult" (Mentor Manual 2000 Friends)

Student Transition and Recovery Program, Inc. (S.T.A.R.) housed in Moultrie Georgia primarily addresses the needs of middle school students who commit offenses that warrant suspension from school or juvenile detention facilities (Stancil, Charles). Students remain in the community and attend their regular assigned schools. The program originated in 1993 in Conroe, Texas.(Kattner, 1996). One of the goals of the program is to enable individual offenders to remain in school while reducing their disruptive behavior. Another goal is to utilize school expulsion as a sanction only after the methods of dealing with the student have been exhausted. Also include in the goals of the program are improvement of the classroom performance, coordinate the efforts of the school and the department in dealing with troubled youth and instill a sense of pride and self discipline in program participants. There are four levels of the S.T.A.R. program. Level one is a 24-week program for students referred by a juvenile court for committing a detainable offense. The degree of involvement for the level one program is seven days per week. Level two S.T.A.R. program lasts six weeks for students for students committing school offenses and referred either by the school or juvenile court. Degree of involvement is school days. Level three S.T.A.R. program is a two-week program for students committing school offenses. Referring Agency for level three S.T.A.R. can be school, parent or law enforcement. Level three students are involved in the program in the morning and the afternoons. Level four S.T.A.R. program is a one-day program for committing a school offense. Referring agency can be school, parents or law enforcement. Degree of participation is morning and afternoons. Parental responsibility is a key component of the S.T.A.R. program.

Refercences

Kattner, C. (1996, January) Keeping Juvenile Offenders in School and in Their Homes while Rehabilitating Them. <u>Middle School Journal</u> (pp. 26, 27, 31).

Mentor Manuel 2000 Friends, pp. 1, 3

Mitchell County Children and Youth, Inc. (1996). The Mitchell County Children & Youth Collaborative. [Brochure]. Bostick, Jenny: Executive Diretor.

Mitchell County Children and Youth, Inc. Case Management Program. [Brochure]. Bostick, Jenny: Executive Director

Mitchell County Children and Youth, Inc. MCCY Mental Health Program. [Brochure]. Bostick, Jenny: Executive Director.

Mitchell County Children and Youth, Inc. Mitchell County Youth Advisory Council. [Brochure]. Bostick, Jenny: Executive Director.

Mitchell County Children and Youth, Inc. Prevention Program. [Brochure]. Bostick, Jenny: Executive Director.

Mitchell County Children and Youth, Inc. Mentoring Program. [Brochure]. Bostick, Jenny. Executive Director.

Mitchell County Children and Youth, Inc. Youth Experiencing Success. [Brochure]. Bostick, Jenny: Executive Director.

Mitchell County Children and Youth, Inc. Postponing Sexual Involvement. [Brochure]. Bostick, Jenny: Executive Director.

Student Transition And Recovery Program, Inc. S.T.A.R. [Brochure]. Stancil, Charles: S.T.A.R. Coordinator.

Chapter 17

The Full Service School: A Holistic Approach to Effectively Serve Children in Poverty

America's children will make or break America's greatness and future. One in four current Americans is a child. Children are the future tense of our humanity. Its quality will depend largely upon our present-tense care of them.
Marian Wright Edelman

Beryl Watnick Ph.D.
Miami-Dade County Public Schools

Arlene Sacks Ph.D.
Union Institute

An examination of issues impacting children in poverty and their chances for success in life, lead to the conclusion that that there is a critical need for a central point where active collaboration between schools, families and communities can take place. The logical site for this to come about is in the neighborhood schools. A revisit to what schools provide leads to the conclusion that a Full Service School offers a physical plant and the opportunity to expand curriculum to meet the basic needs of children in poverty.

"The official poverty rate for young children -23 percent- is more than double the rate of poverty among the elderly and among adults ages 18-64 (both were 11 percent in 1996)". (National Center for Children in Poverty, 1998). All children have the right to share in the dream of complete and authentic participation in American society. An established pattern of disadvantage stands as an overwhelming barrier to equal access. Weissbourd (1996) writes that "many Americans define poverty as simply living in a poor neighborhood or belonging to a mythologized underclass or 'culture of poverty' that is populated with long-term welfare recipients who have lost their moral bearings." Huston, McLoyd, & Coll (1994) cite different categories of economic hardship. "The most common is poverty defined by cash income using the federal poverty threshold as a marker." It is a status that cuts across a diverse population and can fundamentally deprive children of the basic nutrients for hope. Poverty, as an isolated risk factor, does not impair opportunity and achievement.

Variables Effecting Young Children Living in Poverty
" An African proverb tells us that it takes a village to raise a child. We no longer have many villages in the United States, but parents cannot manage to raise children in modern societies without substantial help of others. In villages and families the bases for giving or asking for help seem transparent, "natural," explanations unneeded. We help because family members and neighbors are part of our responsibility and equally because we ourselves may need help from them. Part of the very definition of a stranger is that we have no responsibility for this person (Gordon,1994).

Civic engagement is another aspect that cannot be overlooked when examining effective educational strategies in reaching children of poverty. Blueprint 2000 addresses the critical role of partnerships between parents, businesses, governmental and community agencies that need to be developed in order to effectuate positive change community-wide. Schools and families cannot function in isolation if we are to impact student achievement. Communities and schools must collaborate to prepare children and families for their children's future success in school. This notion takes the position that we can no longer be a nation of egocentric individuals who focus solely on our own nuclear families. We cannot afford to ignore "other people's children". The Children's Defense Fund (1997) reports that:

- Every day 1,407 babies are born to teenage mothers
- Homicide is the leading cause of death for children under 4; every seven hours a child dies at the hands of his/her caregiver
- Every day 8,493 children are reported abused or neglected
  - Thirty percent of all crime is committed by juveniles
  - Children are the fastest growing segment of the criminal population; every 4 minutes a child is arrested for an act of violence.

Communities must work together with the school system to minimize the barriers that impair children from learning and sharing in the bounty this country harvests. It is not only a moral issue but an economic one as well.

Children of Poverty

In 1993, 22 percent of this country's children under the age of 18 lived in families whose incomes were below the federally established poverty line (Weissbourd, 1996). One quarter of all children under the age of 4 live in poverty (The Children's Defense Fund, 1997). The Children's Defense Fund data book for 1997 cites the United States as the first nation in defense spending but the eighteenth in the percentage of children living below the poverty line. With this percentage rating, the U.S. stands as the worst of all the industrialized nations. "We are first in military technology and military exports but twelfth in mathematics achievement and seventh in science achievement of thirteen years olds among fifteen industrialized nations. While we are the top producers of health technology, we are eighteenth in infant mortality and nineteenth in the percentage of our babies born at low birth weights. Our rates of incarceration and child abuse are unparalleled in the Western world" (Karr-Morse & Wiley, 1997).

Poverty cuts across all cultural divides. It is a status exclusive to no single group. Weissbourd (1996) cites that in 1993 approximately 40% of poor children were white, 25% were Hispanic, and 33% were African American. Poverty can be the by-product of under-education, divorce, family illness, and single parenthood. However, as a condition alone, poverty does not predict failure to achieve in school. The negative community and family dynamics can interact to place a young person in jeopardy of school failure.

The startling number of infants born into environments of hunger, neglect and drug abuse in our country is a national disgrace." Pre-term gestation and the resulting low birth weight infant are major contributing factors to infant morality in the first year of life. Because these conditions are predominant among infants born to impoverished mothers, the infant morality rate of the poor is significantly higher than that of the general populace"(Oberg, 1995).

Of further concern are those infants born to teen mothers. While the teen birth rate has fallen over the past ten years, too large a number of young girls are still having babies. "Teen pregnancy is a major contributor to, as well as a consequence of, the poverty that victimizes more than 14 million American children" (Children's Defense Fund, 1998). Healy (1990) states that these teen parents are particularly vulnerable because their "own brains lack both a history of adequate nurturance and the final strokes of nature's maturational brush. These parents are ill-equipped to provide for even their children's most basic physical needs, much less their intellects."

Garbarino (1997) believes that today's children are "most vulnerable to the negative influence of an increasingly socially toxic environment." Garbarino has attached the label of "socially toxic environment" to conditions that are the "social equivalent" to pollution and pesticides. He identifies violence and poverty as socially toxic conditions that place America's children "at risk". Greenspan, Seeley, & Niemeyer (1994) conducted a series of interviews with twenty-five New York City school principals. The findings from this study support Garbarino's assessment. The principals participating in this study unanimously agreed that educators must address the emotional problems of their students if they are to effectively educate them. These principals found that there are insufficient support services resulting in critical needs of children being left unattended. In order to facilitate learning for these young people, support must be provided that will "counter some of the traumatic effects inner-city life can have on children and permit them to achieve more educationally" (Greenspan et al., 1994). Garbarino's solution to educating children exposed to such conditions is grounded in the "human rights perspective on child development." Society must examine what children need to reach their full potential. We must examine issues that relate to the "whole child" without ignoring the context of the child's family." Psychosocial and emotional factors hinder the cognitive and developmental process of poor children" (Oberg,1995).

School Readiness

An issue of significance facing this country's educational system is the question of readiness. Making children ready for school is a national educational goal. The readiness issue is gaining a great deal of attention because teachers are reporting that students from poor, socially depressed neighborhoods are entering school without the requisite skills needed to be successful in kindergarten. Kindergarten teachers are being provided with remediation strategies for their entering five year olds. Problems of verbal fluency and inability to pay attention are being observed in far too many kindergarten students. At the other end of the spectrum, Hamburg (1994) states that "14% of all 17 year olds in the United States can be considered functionally illiterate, and functional illiteracy rates among minority students are well above that level. Each year about 700,000 students drop out of school."

In the Report of the Readiness Committee of Governor Chiles' Commission on Education (1998), it is reported that "For many of Florida's poorest, for the least educated, and for those whose family lives are least stable, the gaps in the state's early childhood programs doom their children to similar lives of underachievement." Research in the field of Early Childhood Education points to the substantial effects early childhood programs have on children's lives years after their participation in such programs (The Future of Children, 1995). The preschool experience can offset the physical, cognitive, social and emotional weight conditions of poverty can place on a child. "The educational boost that preschool provides is particularly important for the one-quarter of Hispanic families that are poor by Federal guidelines." (Schwartz, 1996). The exposure to bilingual education during the earliest years is particularly significant in terms of readiness.

Lack of readiness has significant social and economic implications for our country as a whole. Costly, and often avoidable, special education services, school failure, remediation, low wages, less taxes paid, and higher crime rates are the products of children entering the "system" lacking the skills necessary for transition into school. The availability and quality of early childhood services provided by the "system" become increasingly important for low-income families and their children. Education does not begin in Kindergarten. The "system" needs to extend its services to children from birth to five and coherent collaborative partnerships are needed to ensure quality and accessibility. A child is made particularly vulnerable when poverty interacts with factors such as divorce, single parenthood, parental isolation, parent under-education, community apathy and neglect and abuse. Such traumatic, underlying stressors indicate that a significant portion of children coming into today's classrooms have basic needs that must be addressed before they can successfully attend, interact and achieve in the school environment. A child's learning is greatly impaired by hunger, fear, and anxiety. An effective teacher can no longer be confined to the role of educator. In order to enhance student achievement in disadvantaged communities, teachers need to think "outside the lines" and redefine their own job descriptions. They need to be educators, social workers, and child/family advocates. Teachers and schools need to learn how to attend to the "whole child" within the context of the "whole family". "For every child at risk, there's also a family at risk" (Rubin in Clinton, 1996).

An Alternative: The Full Service School

The 1994 Federal initiative Goals 2000: Educate America Act affirms this philosophy with clearly stated goals for the country's children and families. This act mandates a program of education reform that advocates and supports grassroots efforts for school communities. The fundamental concept of the Full Service School is grounded in the language of Blueprint 2000. As a movement, it incorporates several goals. Some of the goals addressed within the Full Service philosophy include:

- Readiness for school
- Safe learning environments
- Adult literacy
- Parental participation

The Full Service School reaches out into the community to create a bridge between families and schools with the goal of better serving the "whole child".

With overcrowded classrooms and imperfect academic settings, teachers need the appropriate support in order to impact student achievement. Parental participation and community involvement are critical to positive change. As approximately 90% of school-age children spend more than one third of their waking lives within the walls of public schools and 19% of children drop-out of school today (Weissbourd, 1996), there is a need to examine the paradigm for servicing these children and maximizing their opportunities for success in school.

Neuroscience research findings point to the crucial interplay of the baby, mother (or primary caregiver) and early environment in the wiring of the brain. The patterns of neuronal connections directly impact development and the ability to learn. (Shore, 1997). "Numerous studies confirm that the mother's responsiveness strengthens the child's learning and sense of self-sufficiency and thereby opens doors to development that would otherwise be closed." (Hamburg, 1994). In the Florida Children's Forum (1997) the Committee for Economic Development concludes that "the nation must redefine education as a process that begins at birth, one which recognizes that the potential for learning begins even earlier, and encompasses the physical, social, emotional and cognitive development of children." Map and Track 1998 reports an increase in states funding infant and toddler programs. There has been an increase from 18 to 24 states within the past two years. These numbers reflect the mobilization of communities to provide services for this population and maybe a direct response to the public awareness of brain research and the importance of the first three years of life. Since its inception in 1965, the Head Start Program has sought to empower parents in the educational process of their children. The significant impact of parental involvement reaches far beyond the first three years of life. It is often the "single common denominator among successful educational programs for all children" (Lewis, 1993).

Parents cannot be ignored in the equation of their children's education. In 1968 African American psychiatrist and educator, James Comer started developing an educational model that would alter the fundamental structure of schools. Comer's model sought to attend to the whole child, and that child's family. Parental engagement is one of the most noted accomplishments in Comer's design. Comer's School Development Program approach has since been adopted by more than 600 schools across the country. (Clinton, 1996).

Educational achievement becomes compromised when children come to school burdened with complex and debilitating problems. Poverty, divorce, poor health and nutrition, family unemployment are conditions that require concurrent attention of a variety of disciplines. The public school setting is the natural site for the provision of a continuum of health, education and human support services. It is "the place where all of the related activities for student achievement occur" (Division of Full Service Schools, Miami-Dade County Public Schools, 1995). Social service and academic needs of children cannot be separated from those of the family. The Full Service School puts this philosophy into practice. The concept of the Full Service School is based on the premise that every child can learn and that the school can serve as a central resource for meeting the needs of a community's population, from birth to the elderly. The Full Service School Initiative is a holistic response to the unmet needs of today's poorest school children. This initiative is grounded in the philosophy that every child can learn and that the family is the most critical element in the learning process.

Expanded Early Childhood and Adolescent Programs as Part of the Full Service School

Early Childhood advocates have emphasized the critical role the parent plays as the child's first teacher. Head Start successfully put this theory into practice over thirty years ago. With the expansion of Head Start to include Early Head Start (children from birth to the age of 3), the U.S. Department of Health and Human Services, Administration on Children, Youth and Families, extends comprehensive services to even more children born into at risk conditions. Research supports that programs which provide early intervention and prevention services pay for themselves over time. Thus, inclusion of children 0-3 and 3-5 is provided by government funding and laws. At the other end of the spectrum, schools are already providing after school care for older children in the form of learning and study centers, extra- curricular activities, sports and enrichment activities.

The needs of the adolescent are on the front page of newspapers everyday. "The notion that schools should be safe havens is a concept that has found support in law throughout the history of public schools for teachers to teach and children to learn, there must be a safe and inviting educational environment"(Curio,1993).

A Full Service School is a viable option that appears to have positive implications.

The Full Service School creates a "user friendly" environment in which families can look to their local school site as a "one-stop" shop to access coordinated, comprehensive services that meet their own, individual needs. It establishes a holistic approach that targets all the risk factors that serve as barriers to student achievement in low-income communities.

By creating a cohesive collaboration between the neighborhood school and comprehensive community agencies/entities, the Full Service School empowers parents to become their own agents for change. Significant numbers of families who live in poverty are disenfranchised from the educational process. In addition, there are far too many families who seek assistance and often go unserved.

There is a need for a shift in paradigm in which family strengths are built upon and risk factors are addressed through the coordination and delivery of support services that contribute to the nurturing and healthy development in children of all ages. The school site is the most effective point of delivery as each school is "shaped by interaction of geography, history, economics, government, and population" (Calfee & Wittwer, 1995).

The Full Service School- Meeting the Needs of Children in Poverty
> A full service school means a school which serves as a central point of delivery, a single "community hub", for whatever education, health, social/human, and/or employment services

have been determined locally to be needed to support a child's success in school and in the community. Such a school is locally planned and designed to meet the holistic needs of students within the context of their families. The full service school becomes a family resource center, a "one stop service center," for children and families, and where appropriate, for people in the surrounding community. (Interagency Workgroup on Full Service Schools, 1992)

The Full Service School is a term that was coined in 1991 when the Florida legislature passed statute 402.3026. This legislation supports the establishment of partnerships between the State Board of Education and the Department of Health and Rehabilitative Services for the purpose of identifying and meeting the needs of at risk students. (Dryfoos, 1995). The intent of the statute was that by the 1995-1996 school year, these agencies would "jointly establish Full Service Schools to serve students from schools that have a student population that has a high risk of needing medical and support services" (Reynolds, 1992).

The foundation for all programs is the coordination of diverse agencies to provide integrated education, health, and social services to eligible families. The Full Service School is an umbrella term that encompasses a variety of models. They may also be called family resource centers, school-based health centers, or community schools. Regardless of the label, their mission is to eliminate barriers to student achievement through programs designed to involve children and parents on the school grounds. The Full Service School seeks to create a "one-stop" shop at a school that will meet the needs of the diverse population that community serves. These programs often include the following: school readiness; parent education; life skills; adult basic education; teen pregnancy groups; dropout prevention; and substance abuse programs. (Burnett, 1994).

Partnerships in a Full Service School

As every community has its own unique characteristics, there is no distinct blueprint for creating a Full Service School. Creating a Full Service School is an ongoing project that evolves as the needs of the community change. The foundation of the design is poured when specific questions are answered:

- Who will be the stakeholders in the community's school?
- What are the unique needs of your community?
- What services need to be provided to respond to these needs?
- Where will these services be housed?
- When will they be delivered?
- How can the program ensure that services are delivered in a cohesive and effective manner?

A Full Service School should reflect best practices in community partnerships. "Where collaboration is real, you are likely to find principals who are willing to lead and take some risks. They understand that the school alone cannot do the job of helping all children succeed, and that sharing this responsibility means forging partnerships built on reciprocity, in which the school exchanges information, services, support, and benefits with its families and communities." (Davies, 1996). Greenspan et al.'s (1994) research conducted with twenty-five inner city school principals indicates that poverty is the number one social problem their students deal with on a regular basis. One principal in the study stated "help is needed to deal with the child who has the intellectual ability to cope but hasn't got the emotional stability to deal with the classroom situation." All of the principals in Greenspan's study indicated that there were "too many children in special education classes who could be handled in regular classes if there were enough helping services." The researchers concluded that schools need a comprehensive approach when implementing strategies to enhance learning. Mental health and social services play a key role.

The urban school teacher can also make a valuable contribution to solidifying partnerships that empower families. "Teachers in urban schools across the United States are finding themselves at the center of a vast web of interconnected social problems. Far from being able to concentrate on the singular task of educating their students, teachers are also being called upon to act as brokers for a diverse array of social and health services" (Burnett, 1996). By having services available right on site, "student focused" communication is enhanced and support can be easily facilitated. Too often teachers are overwhelmed by the problems that surface in today's classrooms. A teacher who lacks the appropriate support services (on site social workers, school counselors etc.) may start a cycle of improperly labeling children as "hyperactive", "problematic", or "slow learners". Teacher expectation is a key factor in student success. Weissbourd (1996) points to these tags as prophesies that, too often, become self-fulfilling. By extending a student's involvement with other "helping" professionals on the school campus, both children and staff are benefiting.

Key to the success of these cooperative relationships is the establishment of common goals and desired outcomes and the extent and integrity of these collaborations. They must be clearly structured so as to avoid fragmentation and duplication of services. Ongoing communication between community stakeholders and defined interagency agreements can minimize barriers to an effective service delivery plan. Sharing a facility eliminates obstacles and allows for more practical use of space and increases opportunities for the sharing of information. A Full Service Coordinator can further facilitate the effective operation of a "one stop" shop.

As stated earlier, the status of poverty brings with it accompanying problems that create an adverse environment for healthy growth, development and academic achievement. The services provided in each distinct school community must be in response to a community needs assessment. Every community is shaped by its own particular economic status, geographic location and population. Cultural sensitivity and relevance is key in the provision of support services.

Issues of health, parenting, school readiness, teen pregnancy are only some of the needs that require attention in a school-linked program. Parents play a pivotal role in educating their children. With two-thirds of homeless parents never having graduated from high school, completing or continuing their own education and gaining the basic skills essential for independent living greatly enhances the likelihood that they will become effective teachers for their children (Homes for the Homeless, 1992, as cited in Nunez, 1998). More importantly, parents who embrace education may be better able to promote their children's intellectual growth and academic achievement (Nunez, 1998). Full Service School educational programs may include adult basic education, English for Speakers of Other Languages, tutoring, and parenting classes. Datcher-Loury (1989 in Renchler, 1993) suggests that "programs aimed at altering parental behavior may be useful in helping to overcome the effects of economic disadvantage on children's scholastic achievement." Family Literacy Programs such as Even Start may also be made available through the Full Service Schools. School related services include before/after school care, infant/toddler stimulation activities, and gang intervention.

Health care is a critical need in Full Service communities. Kozol (1997) wrote of an elementary school in the South Bronx where reading scores are below those of suburban schools. He points to three reasons for low performance: poverty, physical illness, and hunger. Children cannot learn if they are frightened, hungry and sick. By establishing a clinic on the school site, children's most basic needs can be quickly addressed. Health and nutrition education programs can empower parents and students to make choices that will positively impact their health. Dryfoos (1995) states the need for health care is so dramatic that in 1995 there were approximately 700 school-based clinics as compared to the 10 that existed in 1984. "More than half a million students are receiving free primary health care that is convenient, confidential, and caring. In centers with mental health personnel, substantial numbers of students and their families are gaining access to psychosocial counseling. The demand is overwhelming, especially for mental health services, substance abuse treatment, and dentistry." (Dryfoos, 1995).

By linking schools with social support services, traditional barriers are eliminated and families begin to view their neighborhood school as a hub for "inclusion" rather than "exclusion". In far too many communities across the country there are few interactions between family and schools. A change in the education and social service paradigm calls for a "whole family" philosophy. A family's basic needs must be looked at in relation to their children's achievement in school. The creation of a Full Service School partnership program that collaborates with community agencies can provide families with critical information regarding issues of housing, legal rights, employment assistance, WIC (Women/Infants/Children) and WAGES. By effectively coordinating efforts and delivering services, community agencies can contribute to the elimination of basic barriers to family empowerment.

Schools and communities must work together to mitigate environmental conditions that place our children at risk of school failure. Children must be seen in the context of family and family in relation to community. As a nation, we cannot afford to lose the positive contribution of so many because the "system" has failed. It is not only a humanistic choice, but an economic one as well. Marian Wright Edelman, founder of the Children's Defense Fund, stated "The future which we hold in trust for our own children will be directly shaped by our fairness to other people's children".

Economic hardship takes its toll on children's ability to learn and reach their full potential. Education reform now demands that we shift our perspective on how we teach our children and emphasizes the need to integrate social and educational services so that we can truly meet the needs of today's children. Boundaries must be removed that have historically placed neighborhood schools in isolation of the populations they serve.

We can no longer afford to treat a child's "learning difficulties" in isolation. The "whole child" must be considered before individual learning needs are assessed. The environmental landscape in which that child develops and functions is the defining element in that child's ability to achieve. Garbarino (1997) states that "the key to detoxifying the social environment and to strengthening children to resist it lies in a human rights perspective on child development." He stresses the need to examine what children must have in order to grow and development to their full potential.

"I wish that we could do away with the notion of the school as a fortress against the community and think of it as a bridge into the community." (Kozol, 1997) The Full Service School creates that bridge by establishing true community partnerships with the common vision of nurturing growth and development in children through coordination and integration of services on the school campus.

References

Burnett, G. (1994). Urban Teachers and Collaborative School-Linked Services.

ERIC Clearinghouse on Urban Education, New York; National Education Association, Washington, D.C.

Calfee, C. & Wittwer, F. (1995). Building a Full Service School Florida Department of Education: Florida.

Children's Defense Fund. (1998). The State of America's Children Yearbook 1998. Children's Defense Fund: Washington, D.C.

Clinton, H. R. (1996). It Takes a Village: And Other Lessons ChildrenTeach Us. Simon and Schuster: New York.

Curcio, J. & First. P. (1993). Violence in the Schools. Corwin Press Newbury Park, California.

Davies, D. (1996). The tenth school. Principal. Vol. 76; n. 2; Nov 1996; p. 13-16.

Garbarino, J. (1997). Educating children in a socially toxic environment. Educational Leadership, v. 54, n. 7, p. 12-16.

Gomby, D. (1995). Long term outcomes of early childhood programs: Analysis and recommendations. The Future of Children, vol. 5, n. 3, Winter 1995.

Gordon, L. (1994). Pitied but Not Entitled. Harvard University Press: Cambridge, Mass.

The Governor's Child Care Executive Partnership Board. (1997) Maximizing Florida's Brain Power: A New Vision for Early Care and Education in Florida. Florida Children's Forum: Tallahassee.

Greenspan, R., Seeley, D.S., & Niemeyer, J.H. (1994). Principals speak: The need for mental health and social services Equity and Choice. vol.10, n. 3, p. 19-27.

Hamburg, D. (1994). Today's Children. Times Books: New York.

Hamburg, D. (1994). Today's Children. Times Books: New York.

Healy, J. (1990). Endangered Minds: Why Children Don't Think and WhatWe Can Do about It. Touchstone: New York.

Huston, A., Mcloyd. V. & Coll, Cynthia. (1994. Children and poverty: Issues in Contemporary research. *Child Development*, v65, n.2, April.

Interagency Workgroup on Full Service Schools. (1992). A concept paper. Florida Department of Education. Tallahassee.

Karr-Morse, R & Wiley, M. (1997) Ghost from the Nursery The Atlanta Monthly Press: New York

Kozol, J. (1997). Reflections on resiliency. Pricipal, V.77, n 2., November 1997, p. 5-8.

Lewis, M.C. (1993) Beyond Barriers: Involving Hispanic Families in the Education Process. National Committee for Citizens Education: Washington, D.C.

National Center for Children in Poverty (1998). New & Issues, v 8. N. Spring. Columbia School of Public Health: New York

Nunez, R. (1998). Access to success: Meeting the educational needs of homeless children and families. From the report Homes for the Homeless: New York City.

Oberg, C. (1995). A portrait of America's children: The impact of poverty and a call to action. Journal of Social Distress and the Homeless, vol. 4, n 1, pp. 43-56.

Renchler, R. (1993). Poverty and Learning ERIC Disgest: Clearinghouse on Educational Management: Oregon.

Reynolds, Joseph. (1992). Educational outcomes of a community-based full service school. Paper presented at the Convention of the University Council for Education Administrators. (Minneapolis, MN, October 31, 1991

Schwartz, W. (1996). Hispanic preschool education: An important opportunity. ERIC/Clearinghouse on Urban Education Disgest, n. 113.

Shore, R. (1997) Rethinking the Brain. Families and Work Institute; New York.

Weissbourd, R. (1996). The Vulnerable Child. Addison-Wesley Publishing Company Reading. Massachusetts.

Chapter 18

Fate of the World's Children: A Global Challenge

Estela C. Matriano, Ed.D.
Cincinnati Ohio

It takes a village to raise a child (Clinton, 1996). This paper will demonstrate what it takes a **global village** to help the world's children live a life of dignity. Because the world that we are defining for our children for the next millennium is increasingly becoming globalized due to the rapid development in technology and education, we must educate them how to live in a highly interdependent and interconnected world. Furthermore, it defines for us a teaching approach that requires a globalized perspective in order to face the challenge of helping educate children for a functional and effective world citizenship. It is obvious that there is profound connection between the fate of our children and the progressive development of our global village as it impacts on them as the "inheritors" of this one and only planet earth. (Ward & Dubos, 1972)

This paper is intended to address two major issues:
1. The state of the world's children which undoubtedly determine their fate in the global village.
2. Facing the challenge: Global efforts focused on an educational reform that is aimed at the improvement of the quality of life of the world's children.

It is not easy to be a child in this world which is continuously becoming complex and torn apart by many forces that can easily impinge in the youthful existence of today's children. Likewise it is not easy to be engaged in the education of this children as it requires a mastery of a complex world under the rubric of globalization. It is a challenging concept but one that is exciting and appropriate for education in the third millennium. We are living in global village that is becoming smaller everyday with world events having an impact on our daily lives like "neighborhood happenings." This synergy does not leave us room for isolation and indifference. Instead, it enriches our experience of living in a world without borders and encourages us to be part of the total human drama..

II. The State of the World's Children:

"The United Nations Children's Fund (UNICEF) issues a State of the World's Children report every year. The following summary of the 1993 report signal a break through in the post Second World War period. Since the end of the Second World War, average real incomes in the developing world have more than doubled; infant and child death rates have been more than halved; average life expectancy has increased about a third; the proportion of the developing world's children starting school has risen to more than three quarters; and the percentage of rural families with access to safe water has increased from less than 10% to almost 60%. "In the decade ahead, a clear opportunity exists to make a breakthrough against what might be called the last great obscenity - the needless malnutrition, disease, and illiteracy that still cast a shadow over the lives, and the futures of the poorest quarters of the world's children." The State of the World's Children, 1993 (UNICEF, 1994).

Admittedly, the progress made in improving the life of the world's children in the post World War II era is not enough to meet their basic needs and solve their problems to the extent that they can live a "normal" childhood. Therefore the cause of meeting the most basic needs of all children must be taken up with a new determination as an essential step in solving the problems that afflict the precious human resources of the world society and the hope of the future of humanity.

If we wish to succeed in helping the world's children face their future with hope and with a strong resolve to meet the challenge of life in the next millennium, we need a clear understanding of their problems and their struggles. The UNICEF annual reports and other related publications provide a continuous discussion or the prevailing problems that have yet to be resolved now and in the coming years. The following is a review of some of the major problems as they impact on children's lives world wide. This is intended to provide a knowledge base which can help teachers understand the plight of the world's children, design a relevant curriculum and adopt teaching approaches that will help them get the education that they deserve.

- **Children in conflicts.** The strife of children as children of and in war were reported in the 1996 and 1998 annual reports as a "global black eye." There are around 300,000 children in 1998 who bear the worst of civil strife in the world's war torn nations (1998). Related to the danger of exposing children to war-torn areas is the scourge of landmines. Almost every hour, somewhere around the globe, an anti-personnel landmine deprives a child of sight, limbs of life itself. Some 110 million mines are in the ground, a for every 12 children. (UNICEF, 1998). Where there is a conflict, children are in the middle of it and most often used as human shield or conscripted as child soldiers.

- **Child labor.** This is a new topic on voices of youth web site (edevnews, November, 1997). There is so much abuse recorded about child labor and to stop it requires a concerted effort. It is another crime committed against childhood and human dignity of the young population in the world society. In the developing world, South Asia's working children make up around 60% of the 250 million children ages 5 and 14 who hold jobs. Taking on work includes any schooling for many of these children. (UNICEF, 1991).

- **Malnutrition.** It was reported in 1998 that malnutrition continues to be a silent emergency and an invisible one that is affecting heavily the children in all parts of the world and it imperils women, families and ultimately the viability of the whole societies. It has profound and frightening implications for children, society and the future of humankind (1998). Related to malnutrition is the rampant exposure of the world's children to diseases (i.e. diarrhea, cholera, tetanus, polio, etc.) as they are exposed to unhealthy and dangerous environments. It is not only a problem of hunger but a problem of having the right kind of food/nourishment to sustain the children's health and well being.

- **Sexual exploitation and child prostitution.** A growing problem which is becoming more complex because they are closely linked to deepening economic crisis and social corruption in the world society. The spread of HIV/AIDS and globalization have led to increase in exploitation. Children are the great losers in this sexual exploitation and prostitution because they lose their childhood and dignity at an early stage of human development. Parents and adults in the community need to be educated that this kind of trade can lead to the annihilation of children.

- **Illiteracy.** There are nearly a billion people who are functional illiterates in the world today which includes 130 million school age children, 73 million of them girls who are growing up in the developing world without access to basic education (UNICEF, 1999). This is an overarching problem that could have been a solution to most problems if the world's children are not denied the right to education. Education is the powerful tool that can fight illiteracy and enable the children to enjoy full human development. Literacy can help them gain a knowledge and understanding of their environment and help them prepare for a thoroughly "gainful" life in the future.

III. Facing the Challenge:

The challenge for us educators is how to help the world's children attain a common meaningful destiny of human dignity. It is incumbent upon us to help educate the world's children towards this destiny which was guaranteed by the 1989 Convention on the rights of the Child which became a binding international law on September 2, 1990. As a result what were once seen as the needs of children have been elevated to something far harder to ignore: their rights. (UNICEF, 1999). A copy of the Rights of the Child in Appendix A. These rights although guaranteed are not to be abused. They are to be used intelligently with corresponding responsibilities.

The education revolution within the Convention on the Rights of the Child framework as summarized in **The State of the World's Children 1999** (UNICEF, 1999) have five key elements that interweave and reinforce each other. They are:

- **Learning for Life.** To help children develop literacy, numeracy and psychosocial skills and knowledge base that will equip them to be active and effective participants in the events of their lives This calls for curricula and pedagogies that are inclusive of gender, language and culture and economic disparities and physical and mental abilities, and enable children to deal with them in a positive way. Teachers and students need to relate in new ways so that classroom learning becomes a preparation for life. The teacher must be a guide and facilitator and the classroom must be an environment for democratic participation.

- **Accessibility, quality and flexibility.** Education for All is achieved only when it reaches out to the unreached such as the girls, the rural children, ethnic minorities the disabled and the poor. Various means to reach the unreached are being developed around the world such as multi-grade teaching, distance education, flexible and unified systems of education adopted to the local conditions. It should develop measures to overcome the language barriers, provide measures in emergency situations and help counter child labor. These models requires reform in teaching and innovative models of teacher education which should be matched by improved teaching condition and benefits for teachers such as increase in salaries and supplying other needs.

- **Gender sensitivity and girls' education.** Girls are equally entitled to high quality education but are often denied not only in their entry to the school but also to a fair treatment in the classroom by their teachers and boy classmates. This unequal treatment has been reinforced in instructional materials and the importance that teachers give to boys than to the girls. This inequality has been documented by many research studies on gender and education. Teachers and policy/decision makers in this realm should be gender sensitive to treat boys and girls with equal importance. They equally need to be educated in gender studies as part of their staff development program.

- **The State as key partner.** The State must change from being a central authority of power to a key partner in the education revolution. It has to develop a partnership with all sectors of the community who are players in the education revolution. In developing a partnership, the State can still take the lead in the process of mobilizing the forces in the community in all levels to support its educational reform efforts, forged partnership with both the public and private sectors, decentralize its structure in a way that schools are given more power and autonomy in improving education and achieving its goals. The State can no longer dictate from above but must join hands to be an effective partner in reforming schools and accelerating achievements in more visible measures. Thus, an action oriented partnership can evolve.

- **Care for the young child.** This calls for a good knowledge and understanding of child development; learning begins at birth and that the quality of learning in the first two years of a child has long lasting effect; thereby making early childhood care for child growth and development (ECCD) very important in educational programs. It is obvious that child care and early education go hand in hand requiring an educational reform and teaching that is child centered. Educators in all levels need to be conscious of this foundation in learning.

Conclusions

An education reform that is based on the framework of the Rights of the Child is the "rightful" response to the fate of the world's children. It supports the contention in the report The State of the World's Children 1999 (UNICEF, 1999) that education is the best investment for the children's future. The universal declaration of human rights and the rights of the child are covenants which reinforce each other in realizing the "rightful" place of the world's children in the global village.

Educators in general and teachers in particular are challenged to actively participate on the implementation of an educational reform that will uphold the rights of the child thereby making the quality of life for the world's children a healthy and "gainful" existence. It can be a hard road to travel but those of us who chose to be teachers can only reach out and teach those who need us most. If we can do this, then we can honestly say: teaching is a noble profession.

References

Ayala-Lasso. J. (1996). Keynote speech. World Congress Against Commercial Sexual Exploitation of Children. [On-line]. Available: http://www.childhub.ch/webpub/csechome/22ea.htm

Clinton, H.R. (November, 1996). It Takes A Village: And Some Other Lessons Children Teach Us. Touchstones Books.

Editorial (1998). Strife of children a global black eye. Expressnews.com. [On-line].Available:http://www.expressnews.com:80/pantheon/editorial/editorials/27edl.shtr

Matriano, E. (1995). Globalizing education 2000 and beyond: Meeting the challenges and responding to opportunities. Keynote address. World Conference on Teacher Education. Izmir, Turkey.

Matriano, E. (1997). Transformative education for a global society. Paper presented at the NCSS 77th Annual Conference, Cincinnati, OH.

Matriano, E. (1998). The challenge of globalization to diversity training for the third millenium. Keynote address, Conference on Diversity in the Workplace, Cincinnati, OH.

Reardon, B. (1995). Educating for human dignity: Learning about rights and responsibilities. Philadelphia: University of Pennsylvania Press.

UNICEF (1994). The State of the World's Children. United Kingdom. Oxford University Press.

UNICEF (1996). The State of the World's Children. United Kingdom. Oxford University Press.

UNICEF (1998). The State of the World's Children. United Kingdom. Oxford University Press.

UNICEF (1997). Children and work. Edevnews, 8 (1).

UNICEF (1998).The state of the world's children: Focus on nutrition. [On-line]. Available: http://www.unicef.org/sowc98/foreword.htm

UNICEF (1999). The state of the world's children: Education. [On-line]. Available: http://www.unicef.org/sowc99/sw99rite.htm

Ward, B. & Dubos, R. (1972). Only one earth. New York: W. W. Norton & Company, Inc.

SYMPOSIUM SERIES

1. Jürgen Moltmann et al., **Religion and Political Society**
2. James Grace, **God, Sex, and the Social Project: Glassboro Papers on Religion and Human Sexuality**
3. M. Darroll Bryant and Herbert W. Richardson (eds.), **A Time for Consideration: A Scholarly Appraisal of the Unification Church**
4. Donald G. Jones, **Private and Public Ethics: Tensions Between Conscience and Institutional Responsibility**
5. Herbert W. Richardson, **New Religions and Mental Health: Understanding the Issues**
6. Sheila Greeve Davaney (ed.), **Feminism and Process Thought: The Harvard Divinity School / Claremont Center for Process Studies Symposium Papers**
7. A.T.D./Fourth World, **Children of Our Time: Words and Lives of Fourth World Children**
8. Jenny Yates Hammett, **Woman's Transformations: A Psychological Theology**
9. S. Daniel Breslauer, **A New Jewish Ethics**
10. Darrell J. Fasching (ed.), **Jewish People in Christian Preaching**
11. Henry Vander Goot, **Interpreting the Bible in Theology and the Church**
12. Everett Ferguson, **Demonology of the Early Christian World**
13. Marcia Sachs Littell, **Holocaust Education: A Resource Book for Teachers and Professional Leaders**
14. Char Miller, **Missions and Missionaries in the Pacific**
15. John S. Peale, **Biblical History as the Quest for Maturity**
16. Joseph Buijs, **Christian Marriage Today: Growth or Breakdown**
17. Michael Oppenheim, **What Does Revelation Mean for the Modern Jew?**
18. Carl F.H. Henry, **Conversations with Carl Henry: Christianity for Today**
19. John Biermans, **The Odyssey of New Religious Movements: Persecution, Struggle, Legitimation. A Case Study of the Unification Church**
20. Eugene Kaellis and Rhoda Kaellis (eds.), **Toward a Jewish America**
21. Andrew Wilson (ed.), **How Can the Religions of the World be Unified?: Interdisciplinary Essays in Honor of David S.C. Kim**
22. Marcia Sachs Littell et al., (eds.), **The Holocaust Forty Years After**
23. Ian H. Angus, **George Grant's Platonic Rejoinder to Heidegger: Contemporary Political Philosophy and the Question of Technology**
24. George E. Clarkson, **Grounds for Belief in Life After Death**

25. Herbert W. Richardson, **On the Problem of Surrogate Parenthood: Analyzing the Baby M Case**
26. Leslie Muray, **An Introduction to the Process-Understanding of Science, Society, and the Self: A Philosophy for Modern Man**
27. Dan Cohn-Sherbok (ed.), **The Salman Rushdie Controversy**
28. James Y. Holloway (ed.), **Barth, Barmen and the Confessing Church:** *Katallegate*
29. Ronald F. Duska (ed.), *Rerum Novarum*–**A Symposium Celebrating 100 Years of Catholic Social Thought**
30. Franklin H. Littell, Alan L. Berger, and Hubert G. Locke (eds.), **What Have We Learned?: Telling the Story and Teaching the Lessons of the Holocaust: Papers of the 20th Annual Scholars' Conference**
31. Alan L. Berger (ed.), **Bearing Witness to the Holocaust, 1939-1989**
32. G. Jan Colijn and Marcia S. Littell (eds.), **The Netherlands and Nazi Genocide: Papers of the 21st Annual Scholars' Conference**
33. Marion Mushkat, **Philo-Semitic and Anti-Jewish Attitudes in Post-Holocaust Poland**
34. Katharine B. Free (ed.), **The Formulation of Christianity by Conflict Through the Ages**
35. W. Anthony Gengarelly, **Distinguished Dissenters and Opposition to the 1919-1920 Red Scare**
36. John J. Carey (ed.), **The Sexuality Debate in North American Churches 1988-1995: Controversies, Unresolved Issues, Future Prospects**
37. James P. Hurd (ed.), **Investigating the Biological Foundations of Human Morality**
38. Allen E. Hye, **The Moral Dilemma of the Scientist in Modern Drama: The Inmost Force**
39. Will Morrisey, **A Political Approach to Pacifism** (2 Volumes - 39A-39B)
40. LaRae Larkin, **The Legitimacy in International Law of the Detention and Internment of Aliens and Minorities in the Interest of National Security**
41. Brian L. Fife, **School Desegregation in the Twenty-First Century: The Focus Must Change**
42. Paul Leslie (ed.), **The Gulf War as Popular Entertainment: An Analysis of the Military-Industrial Media Complex**
43. Jutta T. Bendremer, **Women Surviving the Holocaust: In Spite of the Horror**
44. George Anastaplo, **Campus Hate-Speech Codes and Twentieth Century Atrocities**
45. David Brez Carlisle, **Human Sex Change and Sex Reversal: Transvestism and Transsexualism**

46. Jack Parsons, **Human Population Competition: A study of the pursuit of power through numbers** (2 Volumes - 46A-46B)
47. Adam Neuman-Nowicki, **Struggle for Life During the Nazi Occupation of Poland**, translated and edited by Sharon Stambovsky Strosberg
48. Christopher G. Hudson, **An Interdependency Model of Homelessness: The Dynamics of Social Disintegration**
49. Michele Chaban, **The Life Work of Dr. Elisabeth Kübler-Ross and Its Impact on the Death Awareness Movement**
50. Englebert Ssekasozi, **A Philosophical Defense of Affirmative Action**
51. Kimmo Kääriäinen, **Religion in Russia After the Collapse of Communism: Religious Renaissance or Secular State**
52. Edward Timms and Andrea Hammel (eds.), **The German-Jewish Dilemma: From the Enlightenment to the Shoah**
53. Victoria La' Porte, **An Attempt to Understand the Muslim Reaction to the Satanic Verses**
54. Elizabeth S. Spragins, **Metaphoric Analysis of the Debate on Physician Assisted Suicide**
55. Alice Duhon-Ross (ed.), **Reaching and Teaching Children Who Are Victims of Poverty**